STOTFOLD
REFLECTIONS

Queen Street, Stotfold.

STOTFOLD REFLECTIONS

Stotfold people in conversation with
Gordon Huckle, Claude Ingrey and Christine Smith
Edited by Christine Smith

EGON
EPL
EGON PUBLISHERS LTD

First published in 1993 by
Egon Publishers Ltd, Royston Road, Baldock, Herts SG7 6NW

Copyright © Egon Publishers Ltd

ISBN 0 905858 88 3

Designed by Nick Maddren
Campion Publishing Services, Baldock SG7 6DB
Typeset by BookEns Ltd, Baldock, Herts.
Printed in England by
Streetsprinters, Royston Road, Baldock, Herts SG7 6NW

Front and back endpapers: V E Day celebrations 1946
Half-title: Cutting the corn, Arthur Castle sitting on the binder, son Humphrey with the horses.
Title spread: Queen Street 1912.
Above: Wedding party, Mr and Mrs Phillip Brown, bride and groom, August 1927.
Page 5: Mrs F Smith receiving the Dr Barnardo's collection boxes, c. 1940.
Page 6: Stotfold Cricket Team, c. 1890.

Contents

Acknowledgements

There are many people who have co-operated to make this book possible; we extend our grateful thanks to them all. In particular, we should like to thank:

Bert Hyde, for his guidance and enormous contribution of factual information gleaned from his vast knowledge of Stotfold's history; Gordon Huckle and Claude Ingrey for the many hours spent gathering the material for this book; Robert Smith, Frances Huckle, Joan Ingrey, Carol Parry for their continued support and enthusiasm and Walter Griffin and Barbara Bowskill for the loan of their large photographic collections.

We are indebted to the following people who allowed us to reproduce their photographs: J. Bandy, B. Boyce, B. Bowskill, P. Brown, R. H. Brown, F. Butcher, J. Chambers, O. Chapman, B. Charles, D. Chellew, C. Childs, E. Darton, R. Day, the late M. Dear, C. Edwards, L. Edmonds, M. Everitt, J. Gadsden, W. Griffin, J. Hallworth, M.A. Hallworth, S. Hare, M. Harris, C. Howard, M. Howard, G. Huckle, B. Hyde, E. Hyde, K. Hyde, C. Ingrey, B. Jeffs, D. Kempson, P. King, O Kitchener, B. Murphy, D. Nisbet, R. Norman, J. Patrick, F. Phillips, S. Pooley, G.A. Preston, M. Randall, I. Roberts, B. Robinson, A. Ryall, R & H Saunders, A. Scott, D. Shepherd, G. Shepherd, J. Smith, the late M. Smith, H.A.M. Stokes, Stotfold Football Club, F. Triplow, J. Triplow, B. Upchurch, P. Yates.

Our grateful thanks go, too, to the many people who provided us with photographs so that we were able to make a selection from over 400 received.

We should also like to acknowledge the co-operation of The Biggleswade Chronicle, who allowed us access to their library of back copies; and The Bedfordshire Record Office who gave us permission to reproduce the Gaol Calendar, 1831, the 1925 Ordnance Survey map and William Hill's handbill.

Whilst every effort has been made to be as accurate as possible, we apologise in advance for any errors which may have inadvertantly occurred.

Foreword

For some time now, the talk of a book about Stotfold has been the theme of much local conversation. To many people whose lives have been spent in Stotfold, this book will truly be a walk down memory lane. Many of the photographs found in its pages will enable recent inhabitants to visualise the village of Stotfold as it was many years ago. Residents of my age, and indeed older, will remember roads such as Dark Lane (now part of Church Road) when it really was a dark lane; Queen Street with its many thatched cottages; and Rook Tree Lane when it was dominated by the full grown elms in the nearby meadows. Areas like the Germs (now Mowbray Crescent), Alex Smith's meadow (now Alexander Road), and the big field called the Mixies, which still retains that name, were marvellous play areas for the boys and girls of the village.

And when I think of the people who were around in my younger days many former parishioners immediately spring to mind, like the local blacksmith, Eustace Ginn, and John Oliver, the smallholder, whose broad village dialect fascinated both children and grown-ups alike. Then there was Mrs Hyde, whose pork products were, to many of us, the treat of the week, and Jamie Hallworth, whose delicious ice cream got many of us queuing with our basin or jug on a Saturday afternoon. Of course, there were others, too numerous to mention here, who will remain with us forever.

What schoolgirl could ever forget Miss Pearson or Miss Rosser, headteachers in the respective eras of Stotfold Girls' School, or Mrs Bonnett of the Infants' Department? The school building, alas, no longer stands. And what boy could forget Mr Viner and Parry Thomas, headteacher and basher of Stotfold Boys' School? The redoubtable Bobby Childs was long before my time.

Stotfold has changed in many respects through the years. Many of us can remember when it was a quiet village and you could play children's games in the street, being disturbed only occasionally to let the milkman, greengrocer, coal merchant or baker through with their horses and carts. Today it is a very busy place with an almost

*Stotfold Football Club supporters
c. 1948*

constant flow of traffic, so that it is almost impossible to walk across some roads without having to hurry.

It has been my privilege to write the foreword for this book, and I would like to pass on my sincere thanks to Christine Smith, Gordon Huckle, Claude Ingrey and John Street for all the work they have put into this project, although I am sure they have found enjoyment in their task.

Finally, I hope that you, the reader, will find much to interest you as you delve through the pages of *Stotfold Reflections* and glimpse into the not too distant past. Now it is up to you to preserve our town, with its worthy heritage, for future generations.

Arthur Castle
Chairman, Stotfold Town Council

Introduction

For a long time the idea of a book about Stotfold had been discussed at the Stotfold Local History Adult Education Class with many people asking if it would ever be produced. During the winter of 1992/3 it was decided that a start should be made and three members agreed to undertake the task. On making enquiries we were told that a definitive history of Stotfold would not be all that popular and, in any case, we already had a good history written by Reverend G.C.H. Phillips. We therefore resolved to do something quite different and so work began on *Stotfold Reflections*.

Our aim was to present a period of Stotfold history in a way that would be of interest to everybody. The main source of the material in the book is recorded conversations with people of Stotfold as they reflected on years gone by. The book also contains a collection of photographs and other relevant items, such as extracts from magazines, which we hope will all serve to give an impression of the life and people of Stotfold from approximately 1850 to 1950. Whilst the book has many characters and much humour, the tragedy of the two world wars is not forgotten. Obviously, since we are dealing largely with living memory, the second half, from 1900 to 1950, will be covered more fully than the first 50 years.

Each chapter focuses on a different subject, but no attempt has been made to cover every aspect of the life of the village. The first chapter sets the scene with a brief history of Stotfold up to 1950, then most of the other chapters and some of the sub-sections open with a short introduction followed by the corresponding extracts from the recorded conversations.

We are grateful to all the people who have shared their memories with us and permitted us to publish them. We are also grateful to the many others who have loaned us old photographs and additional material. Without the help of both these groups this book would not have been possible, but inevitably, due to lack of space, we have been unable to include everything we have received. Finally, our hope is that *Stotfold Reflections* will give pleasure to the reader.

Bedfordshire.

LENT ASSIZE—MARCH 3d, 1831.

GAOL CALENDAR.

SAMUEL CHARLES WHITBREAD, Esquire,

Sheriff.

Alphabetical List of Prisoners for Trial.

NO.	NAMES.	AGE.	OFFENCES.
3.	ALLEN, James	34.	Manslaughter.
22.	Addington, James	17.	Setting fire to a Hay Stack.
17.	Blows, James	26.	House-breaking.
21.	Bunker, James	50.	Sending a Threatening Letter.
25.	Baines, John	19.	Stealing a Fowl.
36.	Betts, Mary	15.	Stealing a Silk Handkerchief.
11.	Cooper, Thomas	41.	Tumultuously assembling, and Conspiracy.
28.	Cutler, William	29.	Stealing Flour.
34.	Cowland, John	18.	Stealing Wheat, &c.
35.	Carter, Thomas	25.	Stealing Fowls.
1.	Deacon, Daniel	18.	House-breaking.
26.	Fuller, William	54.	Sheep-stealing.
27.	Fuller, James	19.	The like.
31.	Foster, John	36.	Stealing Fir Poles.
4.	Grose, William	50.	Sheep-stealing.
13.	Godfrey, William	61.	Tumultuously assembling, and Conspiracy.
15.	Gentle, James	27.	The like.
19.	Gentle, Henry	35.	House-breaking.
29.	Groocock, Barbara Maria	25.	Stealing Wearing Apparel, Trinkets, &c.
32.	Hine, Thomas	28.	Explosion in a Dwelling-house.
23.	Keningale, John	39.	Stealing a Hen.
24.	King, James	40.	Stealing Fagots, &c.
30.	Lock, Henry	48.	Embezzlement.
7.	Megre, James	17.	House-breaking.
12.	Millard, Thomas	24.	Tumultuously assembling, and Conspiracy.
16.	Payne, William	30.	House-breaking.
2.	Rainbow, Thomas	18.	The like.
14.	Reynolds, Robert	21.	Tumultuously assembling, and Conspiracy.
18.	Shaw, John	30.	House-breaking.
20.	Saunderson, William	27.	The like.
33.	Summerfield, William	23.	Stealing Wheat, &c.
6.	Taylor, James	17.	House-breaking.
8.	Underwood, Charles	26.	Sheep-stealing.
9.	Underwood, Benjamin	19.	The like.
5.	Woodcraft, John, (*alias* Gudgeon)	18.	House-breaking.
10.	Whitbread, John	20.	Burglary.

Webb, Printer, Bedford.

Bedfordshire.

LENT ASSIZE—MARCH 3d, 1831.

GAOL CALENDAR.

SAMUEL CHARLES WHITBREAD, Esquire,

Sheriff.

Alphabetical List of Prisoners.

NO.	NAMES.	AGE.	SENTENCE.
3.	ALLEN, James	34.	Two Months, N. H. C. hard Labour.
22.	Addington, James	17.	Acquitted.
17.	Blows, James	26.	Four Months, O. H. C. hard Labour.
21.	Bunker, James	50.	No true Bill.
25.	Baines, John	19.	Three Months, O. H. C. hard Labour.
36.	Betts, Mary	15.	The like.
11.	Cooper, Thomas	41.	Two Months, ditto.
28.	Cutler, William	29.	Six Months, ditto.
34.	Cowland, John	18.	Acquitted.
35.	Carter, Thomas	25.	Four Months, N. H. C. hard Labour.
1.	Deacon, Daniel	18.	Acquitted.
26.	Fuller, William	54.	Eighteen Months, O. H. C. hard Labour.
27.	Fuller, James	19.	Death recorded.
31.	Foster, John	36.	No true Bill.
4.	Grose, William	50.	Death recorded.
13.	Godfrey, William	61.	Twelve Months, O. H. C. hard Labour.
15.	Gentle, James	37.	Death recorded.
19.	Gentle, Henry	35.	Death recorded.
29.	Groocock, Barbara Maria	25.	One Year's Imprisonment, N. H. C.
32.	Hine, Thomas	28.	Acquitted.
23.	Keningale, John	39.	Acquitted.
24.	King, James	40.	Six Months, O. H. C. hard Labour.
30.	Lock, Henry	48.	Acquitted.
7.	Megre, James	17.	Death recorded.
12.	Millard, Thomas	24.	Death recorded.
16.	Payne, William	30.	Six Months, O. H. C. hard Labour.
2.	Rainbow, Thomas	18.	Acquitted.
14.	Reynolds, Robert	21.	Death recorded.
18.	Shaw, John	30.	Six Months, O. H. C. hard Labour.
20.	Saunderson, William	27.	Death recorded.
33.	Summerfield, William	23.	Acquitted.
6.	Taylor, James	17.	Death recorded.
8.	Underwood, Charles	26.	Acquitted.
9.	Underwood, Benjamin	19.	Acquitted.
5.	Woodcraft, John, (*alias* Gudgeon)	18.	Death recorded.
10.	Whitbread, John	20.	Death recorded.

Webb, Printer, Bedford.

---

11. THOMAS COOPER,	41	Committed the 6th December, by WILLIAM HENRY WHITBREAD, Esq. charged with having on Thursday the 2d Day of December last, unlawfully and tumultuously assembled in the Parish of *Stotfold*, and having conspired to obtain, by force and violence, an increase of Wages, and for other unlawful Purposes.
12. THOMAS MILLARD,	24	
13. WILLIAM GODFREY,	61	
14. ROBERT REYNOLDS,	21	
15. JAMES GENTLE,	37	
16. WILLIAM PAYNE,	30	Committed the 6th December, by W. H. WHITBREAD, Esq. charged with having on Thursday the 2d December last, feloniously broken into and entered the Shop of *Benjamin Howard*, at *Stotfold*, and stolen, taken, and carried away one Loaf of Bread, value Sixpence, the Property of the said *Benjamin Howard*.
17. JAMES BLOWS,	26	
18. JOHN SHAW,	30	
19. HENRY GENTLE,	35	
20. WILLIAM SAUNDERSON,	27	

Chapter 1

Stotfold Past

Some early spellings of the name Stotfold have been Stodfold (1007), Statfalt (1086), Stotfold (1199), and Stotfolt (1287). The name may reflect the fact that in former times horses, cattle and sheep were folded in the village on their way along the Great North Road, which forms the eastern boundary of the village.

In late Saxon times the village belonged to Aschel, a thane of King Edward the Confessor who died in 1066. According to the Domesday Book (1086) Stotfold was held by Hugh de Beauchamp. It then formed part of the barony of Bedford. There were 21 villeins, 14 bordars and 6 serfs. From these figures it has been estimated that the total number of inhabitants was 200. There were four water mills in the village assessed at £4 and 400 eels annually.

From Domesday to 1950, agriculture was all important. Early on, this was intrinsically bound up with the manors. There were three Stotfold manors: the large Stotfold Brayes manor, the smaller Stotfold Newnham manor and the Rectory manor, which was smaller still. Until the dissolution of the monasteries (c1540), the three Stotfold manors were owned either by religious houses or great nobles. Stotfold was relatively unimportant to most of these people, and there were no resident lords of the manor in the village during that period. Even afterwards, when the lords of Stotfold manors were of lesser rank they still preferred to live elsewhere. Indeed, the only resident lords of a Stotfold manor seem to have been Edward Butler, his son George and his grandson Beckenham. They were lords of both Stotfold Brays and Stotfold Newnham from 1547 to 1610. Probably they lived in a house where the Bury now stands (Dr Stevenson's house near Randall's mill). Some of the Butlers' names are found in the Stotfold Parish Register. Edward Butler himself left instructions that he was to be buried in Stotfold Parish Church. Eventually when the lords of the manors sold their land, but not their titles, the new owners chose to be absentee landlords. So for long periods the villagers came into contact with no one more important than the tenant farmers. It is often contended by Stotfolders that this led to an independence of spirit in the village.

The Gaol Calendar, Bedford Gaol, 1831, giving details of the Stotfold men involved in the Riots of 1830. (Reprinted with permission from Bedfordshire Record Office.)

The 18th century and the first half of the 19th century was the time of the turnpike trusts and toll gates on the road. The Round House Toll Gate, Great North Road, was built in 1816 and continued operating until 1868 (see appendix).

No history of Stotfold, however brief, would be complete without some reference to the notorious Stotfold Riots that took place in the village in December 1830. In considering this incident it should always be remembered that the conditions of the farm labourers and their families at this time were deplorable. *The Times of London* described the affair as a 'desperate riot'.

The trouble started late on Wednesday night, 1st December, when some disturbance occurred. On the next day, the labourers of the village, armed, for the most part, with clubs and bludgeons, congregated together in the churchyard and at a vestry meeting demanded the dismissal of the assistant overseer, exemption from taxes and the raising of wages to two shillings a day. This last demand was refused, threatening behaviour ensued and some of the farmers were struck. To make matters worse, five men stole a loaf of bread, costing 6d, and a nearby field of uncarted stubble was set alight by the rioters in order to frighten the farmers. Friday was quiet. Then on Saturday afternoon Mr Whitbread J.P. from Southill descended on the village with 100 special constables he had sworn in, plus another 100 from the Lord Lieutenant; in little more than half-an-hour, ten of the ringleaders were apprehended and forthwith committed to Bedford goal. On coming to trial under the savage laws of the time, five of the men were sentenced to death and five were given prison sentences. All the death sentences were later commuted, three of the men receiving prison sentences while the other two, a Mr Gentle and a Mr Saunderson, were transported to Australia for 14 years. Descendants of these two families still live in Stotfold.

From 1850 to 1900 the conditions of the farm worker gradually improved. This was important to Stotfold as agriculture remained the main area of employment until the First World War. Then there was a move away from the land to industry so that, by the early thirties, it seemed as though everybody was cycling to work in the factories of Letchworth or to the Bondor at Baldock.

In the hundred years from 1850 the population of the village increased from 1,395 to 3,979 and the village grew to accommodate the increased numbers. There were seven places of worship namely St. Mary's Parish Church, five non-conformist chapels and the Salvation Army Hall. The Parish Hall was a corrugated iron building erected in 1888 and called affectionately 'the Tin Box'; it was also known as the Temperance Hall.

The village during this period was well provided with public houses. The two schools were simply referred to by the villagers as the Girls' School and Boys' School. There was a good range of shops, albeit well spread out. Industry in the village included at various times, straw plaiting, brick making, coprolite digging, corn milling and brewing. Also during this period, radio and motion pictures made their appearance. Here, as elsewhere, normal life was greatly disrupted by the two world wars. Most of these topics will be dealt with more fully in the chapters that follow.

The '29 Brigade' c. 1919. Unemployed farm labourers working on the road building programme (see appendix).

Chapter 2

A Village Childhood

Schools

As already mentioned the two schools were referred to by the villagers as 'The Girls' School' and 'The Boys' School', but officially they were known as the National St Mary's Girls' and Infants' School and the Roe's Endowed Boys' School.

The Girls' School

Document from the time capsule, discovered in 1992 when the Girls' School was demolished.

St Mary's School was erected in 1843 on the corner of Rook Tree Lane and Mill Lane, the cost being met by subscription. Mr Henry Octavius Roe, a solicitor and Stotfold's most generous benefactor, was the largest subscriber. It was a Church of England school and its windows and doors closely resembled those of a church. The headmistress had her own living quarters and the school building was divided into two rooms by a partition. Despite its being a large and very handsome school, it became necessary to enlarge it in 1853, in 1870 and again in 1890. By 1891 education had been made compulsory and for the first time it was free of charge. This period also saw the introduction of school attendance officers who were to become the scourge of generations of schoolchildren. At the age of seven boys were promoted from the infants' class of the Girls' School to the Boys' School.

Sadly, the school was pulled down in February 1992, but the demolition revealed a time capsule which contained 40 old coins, a stone marked with the date of building, and a list of the names of the vicar, the church wardens, a subscriber, the architect and the workmen who had built the school. These artefacts are now housed in the new St Mary's School.

Schooldays were so different then, as a glance through the log book for 1863–1922 will show. One day in 1872, some of the teachers were sent to round up absentees, and returned having been given such excuses as, 'have gone to plaiting school' or 'can't afford the fees'.

Helping with the harvest was often a reason for keeping the children off school and girls in particular were frequently needed at home to look after the new baby.

But there were unexpected treats, too. In June 1887, the children were given two afternoons off to celebrate Queen Victoria's Jubilee, and in 1904 several children had a day off to see Buffalo Bill in Hitchin.

In winter the classrooms were generally heated by roaring fires which roasted those who sat close by, but hardly touched those unfortunates in the back row. Even so, on a bitterly cold winter's day in January 1912, the indoor temperature dropped to 34°F and ink froze in the ink wells.

No one can talk of the Stotfold Girls' School and do it justice without mentioning Mrs Gertrude Bonnett who was in charge of the infants' department. Born in Stotfold in 1875, the daughter of Mr and Mrs Fred Brown, she was the elder sister of Mrs Lizzie Pateman (Bruce's wife) of Caldicote Manor. In 1886 at the age of 11½ years she was installed as a pupil teacher at the school and became a firm favourite with the children. She retired in 1940 after 53 years' devoted service there, and died in 1965 aged 90 years.

Above: The Girls' School 1906.

Below: Mrs Bonnett, 90 years old in 1965.

As early as 1924 I remember helping to push Mrs Bonnett to and from school in her three-wheeled wicker bath chair. She, like us, lived on The Green. There was never any lack of volunteers. Generations of Stotfolders owed their early schooling to Mrs Bonnett. *Bert Hyde*

Mrs Bonnett, she was a character, I can see her now sitting in the front row at the school concert. Teddy Bowskill, was about five and he had a part, he used to stand there staring at Mrs Bonnett, he couldn't remember his lines unless Mrs Bonnett was sitting there. *Joan Smyth*

When we went to school we used to go and catch hold of a rope behind the Bowman's steam wagon to help us run to school. If the weather was bad in the winter we used to be given about tuppence

Mixed infants class, 1909.

which we spent on twopenn'orth of cheese, and call in and get a little bit of bread from Pearmain's the bakers, for our school dinner. We used to have a Miss Sanders come from Clifton and Jenny Moore, she lived in the School House, I think. Lizzie Pateman, Bruce's wife taught there for a long time. We used to laugh about it when we grew up, because I don't think that any of them were qualified teachers. Miss Sanders, she was a bit funny, we used to go and get the answers out of her book and put them down, and then we'd get a tick to it, but that wasn't helping us, was it? Life was easy during my school days, we used to come home through those meadows and come out by Manor Farm. *Maud Castle neé Seymour*

I hated school, I don't know why. We used to take a big potato every Monday to the Girls' School and put it under the fire. You'd be sitting there and one would go off bang, and you'd think, I hope that's not my potato. When I was 12 years old, (Lizzie Pateman used to teach then) we had the most terrific thunderstorm you ever did, and all Rook Tree Lane was flooded like a river. They had to bring horses and carts, my dad brought one, to carry us out of the school and get us in the carts to come home. It was during a sewing lesson. *Olive Chapman neé Oliver*

We went to the Girls' School, we walked there and back and came home to dinner every day. We used to go the road way and come back the meadow way, or vice versa. Old Jim King used to come after us children with his old thick stick; we hadn't done anything wrong, but he just didn't like school children. He lived in Tythe Cottage. They reckon that top room was haunted. *Phyllis King née Brown*

My school days were wonderful. When I started at six, Mrs Dale was Head, followed by Miss Meskimmon and Miss Pearson. She used to live in a house near the Crown, John Chambers lives there now. She'd come to school with three big Red Setters. Her clothes would touch the floor, I always thought she was a Russian. I was a naughty girl at school – sometimes you repeat what your parents say – I would go home and tell my dad about her and he would say, 'the old Bolshie'. Next time she grumbled at me I said, 'My dad says you are an old Bolshie.' She didn't punish me for that, but I did get a smack when I got home.

She was marvellous with us. When she came she brought boxes and boxes of beautiful dressing-up clothes. We used to go to the Church and do pageants at the Church Fetes, and we also did plays at school.

Miss Pearson was one for sports. You couldn't be in the sports class unless you had a gymslip, and my mother couldn't afford to buy me one. Well I was one of these little girls who was going to get one some how or other. So I looked around for a wealthy person that had got a daughter about my age. You'll laugh now, it was Bessie Smith's mother. I knocked and asked if Bessie had got an old gymslip, 'Oh yes', she said. She would always do anybody a good turn. So mother pressed and cleaned it and I was able to join the class. *Florence Phillips née Gentle*

Gym class, c. 1925; teacher, Miss Pearson, with Randall's mill in the background.

Cinderella being performed by the Girls' School, late 1930s.

Miss Meskimmon used to live in this house, (Silverbirch, The Green) and she used to breed Red Setters. My friend Fred, he had got a stick, and he dared me to touch her pony under the belly. So when she was coming along the road on her way home with her pony and trap, I touched it and made the pony run like 'ell. Well I was for it next morning, did she leather me! *John Chambers*

I really enjoyed school, I was a good scholar, I had to leave when I was 14. There was Miss Meskimmon, and old 'Moggy Four Eyes', she biked from Clifton. She used to wear high neck things with bones in to hold it up, long skirts and boots. She had a bit of elastic attached to her skirt that fixed right round her foot so that as she cycled it didn't lift her skirt. You weren't allowed to show a leg in those days. *Lily Edmonds neé Huckle*

We couldn't go home to dinner from school because we had too far to go. We used to have to take our sandwiches, there was no facilities. On our way to school we used to have to peg out Nobby Gentle's goats. He had 10 goats and we pegged them out all the way up Peewit Road, and when we came home at four o'clock we would take them in, he'd got a great big shed that he put them in.

When we got there in the morning two were picked to stoke the fires up. We had to go right across that school yard and fill the coke up and stoke the fires. The toilets was in the yard. We used to have to stop one night a week to do the inkwells out. One time I pinched some school nibs and mother made me take them back.

We had some good plays at school, I really enjoyed them. We did Cinderella one year. Charlie Bonnett made the coach and it was absolutely marvellous, he did it all in wicker with roses all the way round. Iris Gentle she was Cinderella. Curly Bowskill and me had to dance at the ball. The school was packed. *Peg Humphries née Millard*

The Boys' School

The Boys' School was built in 1808 by Mr Henricus Octavius Roe for boys from poor, Church of England families. The original school was in the master's house, now number 97 Church Road. Later a large separate school building was erected, which is now the Roecroft Centre. In 1818 it was described as 'A school where about 15 to 20 boys were taught at threepence and fourpence a week and the master keeps a night school containing 8 to 20 scholars'. The school was endowed with £20 per annum by Mr H O Roe in 1833. William Hill the master issued a hand bill in 1835, a copy of which has survived, offering to instruct young gentlemen in the 'several branches of English Education, the Classics and Mathematics'.

The log also exists for Stotfold Board School. This was Roe's Endowed School, enlarged and refurnished. It opened on 26 October 1891 by the headmaster, Mr J E Wood, with 133 boys in attendance.

Top: Handbill issued by William Hill, headmaster, in 1835.

Bottom: Roe's Endowed Boys' School, c. 1850, with pupils in the school yard.

EDUCATION.

Wm. Hill begs to announce to the Inhabitants of Stotfold and its vicinity, that he has received the appointment of Master to the School lately built and endowed by Mr. H. O. Roe, in that village; and that he intends, on the 21st of January, 1835, to open it for the instruction of Young Gentlemen in the several branches of English Education, the Classics, and Mathematics, forming a complete course of sound and useful instruction.

Terms.

	£	s.	d.
Reading, Writing, Arithmetic, and Grammar, per quarter	0	15	0
The same with History, Geography, Practical Geometry, and Mensuration	1	1	0

Extras.

	£	s.	d.
Book-keeping	0	10	6
The Classics and Mathematics	1	1	0

Should private instruction, in any of the above branches, be required, W. H. would be happy to comply with the wishes of his friends, by attending them either at the school or at their own residence. He also proposes to make arrangements to receive, after the next Midsummer vacation, a limited number of Boarders.

Paternoster, Printer, Hitchin.

In November 1896, it was recorded that the boys had shown an improvement in military drill, the Upper Standard having thoroughly mastered the 'formation of fours'.

Not all the boys, though, adhered to military discipline as is shown by an entry in May 1899 when Edwin Dear disrupted the singing class by 'repeatedly misbehaving himself'. Refusing to have his hand smacked, he was struck on the back, whereupon he retaliated by kicking the master in the leg. He was supported in this action by his brother who 'shouted out insolently'.

This tale about school goes back to the early 1900s, long before I went there. Well the teachers at that time were not interested in sport, so the pupils formed their own football team and Bruce Pateman was captain. They would play other schools, evenings and weekends. One of the reasons they made Bruce captain was they used to borrow his father's spring cart to take them. And Bruce was one of the very few who always had a bit of pocket money. When they went off for matches in the cart Bruce would stop off at the Queen's Head and buy them all half a pint. *George Turner*

I sat next to John Bigg at school, he said, 'Alf if I give you a ha'penny will you help me with my sums?' So he gave me a ha'penny and I helped him. *Alf Cardell*

If you misbehaved, Bobby Childs used to give you the cane, which was an ash stick, quite thick. You got four or five strokes and didn't do any writing that day. Sometimes he'd send me out into the porch, well he did until I started running home. When I first started school, Nigger told me if I didn't give him one of my biscuits he was going to bash me up. If you got far enough and the teacher thought you knew enough, you could leave school at 12. My brother left school at 12, but I was 14 before I left. *Jack Brown*

Old Bobby Childs used to buy postcards that you paint on with water, it would bring out a colour picture. He would sell them to you for tuppence or thruppence each, and he was none too pleased if you couldn't afford to buy one.

I was always on time in the morning. We used to polish our shoes with black lead to make them shine, you could see your face in mine. I had lots of medals for regular attendance at school. When I left school at 14 I was due for my final attendance medal. I never received that medal until 30 years later when the school master at that time asked if anyone knew of me. My nephew Robert Busby was given the medal to bring to me. *Bert Jeffs*

Some Friday afternoons when I was at school Bobby Childs would say, 'Would you like to go and get me a sack of chickweed?' When he lived in the school house he used to keep 'ens in there. I'd take a sack and go and collect it from one of the fields. *Archie Shepherd*

At the Boys' School there were seven classes and only three

Teachers at the Boys' School, c. 1900. William Childs, headmaster (rear, centre).

Boys' School, 1926.

teachers. There were three rooms – two of the teachers used to take two classes each, that was forms one to four. Then in the big room Mr Childs took classes five and six. And he also had a special class for the 13-year-olds to try and give them a few 'ints as to what would happen when they left school. He used to put them through the hoop and give them harder lessons. The only help he did have, his wife used to come in on Friday afternoons and we always used to have to do drawing. His wife would take that while he did his books. We all had to take our own subject for drawing and painting, it would nearly always be something out of the garden. A carrot one week, an apple the next, then a few pea pods and so on. They used to collect them up at the end of the class and take them home for themselves.

One day I was sitting having breakfast with my father. Childs used to teach him when he was at school. He asked me, 'What's Gaffer Childs learning you now then?' 'At the moment he's giving us a series of lectures on the evils of alcoholism.' My father said, 'He ought, he has his own whiskey delivered from Flitton's in gallon jars'. I suppose I was about nine or ten. *George Turner*

At the Boys' School, there was one boy I felt sorry for because he had a hard life, and when he started working and getting a bit of money together, he was called up in the army and was blown up in a tank. This was Jack Carter. The teachers used to inspect the

Parry Thomas.

children, and the teacher said to him, 'Ain't you got any soap in your house then Carter?' 'No, Sir, I ain't got no coal either.' So the teacher went down to Teddy Dear's the coalman and paid sixpence for one hundredweight of coal for him. That was a teacher called Mr Perriman, he came before Parry Thomas. *Albert Scott*

At the Boys' School in the early '30s we went one night each week to the Cloisters at Letchworth to learn wicker work. In 1931 I bought a carbide lamp from Crawley's shop in Regent Street, where the Post Office is now. On my way to the Cloisters with my new lamp on my bicycle, it went out and a policeman stopped me for having no light. I said it had just gone out and suggested that he felt the top of it, which he did and burnt his fingers. I relit the lamp and carried on my way. *Bert Hyde*

Parry Thomas used to come every day on a little old round-tanked BSA motorbike and we used to play little tricks with this motor bike; we put sugar in the tank and put water in. We thought we'd have an easy time in the classroom because he was fiddling around with his motorbike. Although we played tricks on him, he was a real good teacher. *Reg Saunders*

Parry Thomas always wore spats and he stank of tobacco. He was always going up the Black Lion to see Mr Bigg. He used to take us gardening, we had a school garden up Norton Road. We'd march up there with our spades and forks and we would dig. He'd say 'You carry on boys, I'll catch you up'. Of course he'd go straight up the Black Lion and see Mr Bigg. Then he'd come up about an hour later and say, 'Have you done it?' *John Cramp*

Parry Thomas marked the spot where he wanted these boys to go up and dig this celery trench, but he wouldn't be going there straight away because he had to call in to see Mr Bigg on business. When he got up there all you could see out of this trench were the spades going, it was that deep. *Gordon Huckle*

At school during the winter when a hard frost was expected, they used to let us throw water down in the playground for slides. You had to make sure you didn't have it too close to the wall because people would come along and crash their heads on the wall. They would put the water down last thing at night, hoping that it would be nice and slippery in the morning. *Alan Dear*

Sticker-sole – the reason he was called that was because his father repaired shoes, his real name was Williams. Well, we were at school one day and young Stickers came in and he had long trousers on which were tucked inside his boots. So Parry says, 'Take your trousers out of your socks, boy.' 'Can't, Sir, they 'ang, Sir.' 'What do you mean they hang? all people's trousers hang', Parry made him pull them out and they were all torn, they were obviously hand-me-downs.

Before the war Parry would come out at the end of play time and ring this bell. But during the war bells were banned, because it was used as a gas or fire warning, so he got one of these bulb horns, which he'd taken the bulb off, and would come out and blow that. *John Cramp*

Top: Girls' School, 1946.

Bottom: Boys' School, 1947.

Childhood Memories

Although toys, games and treats were few and far between, childhood was still a time of great happiness. Pleasure was gained from the simplest of pastime activities.

My brother was born in February 1920, it was a beautiful day and we were spinning tops up and down the middle of Regent Street when he was born. There were no motors then. The path along there used to be about two feet above the road. *Bessie Upchurch née Smith*

I was born in Rook Tree Lane. When I was about seven, my sister, Millie, and I were sitting up in bed looking through some texts from the Salvation Army Sunday School, when I saw somebody come through my mother's bedroom wall and go across the bed and out of the window. He looked a bit like Father Christmas because he had got a red cloak with white stripes and he was bearded. My sister and I screamed. Mum told us afterwards that she came running up the stairs to see what was wrong and we both told her the same story.

We used to play hopscotch, spinning a top and trundling a hoop, the girls used to have a stick and the boys used to have an iron with a hook on it. We had wooden hoops and the boys had metal ones. All the boys used to have hob nails in their boots to stop them wearing out and in the winter as they went along the ice you

Rook Tree Lane, showing Rook Tree House, to the left.

would see the sparks fly. In the summer we went out and played in the evening a lot, we played games in the street. We would line up either side of the street and chant, 'The farmer's gone to Devonshire, and won't be home for many a year, so sheep, sheep come home', and then you had to dash across the road without being caught. It was all right then because there was no traffic. *Lily Edmonds née Huckle*

There were about five of us old boys, and, up Mill Path they were growing potatoes at the time and we took one out from each root – we got half-a-dozen potatoes. Well somebody had got a box of matches, I wasn't allowed matches, and lit a bit of a fire. We put these potatoes in and after about ten minutes we ate them, they weren't nowhere near cooked, but they were delicious. But by this time it was getting on for seven o'clock and my mother came up there, she'd heard where we was. She said, 'Come here my boy, come along home', then all the way home from Mill Path she kept clipping me. They don't do that today. *Edward Bowskill*

The girls used to play skipping with a length of rope across the road and if there was a trap come by they used to drop the rope so they could run over it. We also used to play hopscotch in the middle of the road.

Us old boys used to have a reel of cotton, a pin and a button. We used to thread it through the button, tie it and then wind it round the pin and then we used to put it in the putty in the window

Boys playing in the field, c. 1920, now St. Mary's Avenue. St. Mary's Church, Boys' School and Schoolhouse in the background.

frame. We'd get round the corner holding the length of cotton, give it a pull and the button would tap the window; when they come out we used to disappear. *Jack Brown*

We used to have an apron put on us, then we were sent off to go and glean the stuff to feed the few hens we had in the back yard. After the corn had been cut it was put into sheaths and shocks – they used to put us kids on that – and then it would have to stand to ripen, and after they cleared that away, the spilt stuff that was on the ground. You was at liberty to go on the fields and collect it up. We was always given jobs to do, we had to feed the hens and collect the eggs. One time I broke all the eggs on my way home, so when I got to the pond on The Green I washed the bag and told my dad that there weren't any eggs that day. *Maud Castle neé Seymour*

When we were kids, Gordon Day, who lived up the top of Queen Street, and one or two more, used to go and play down Bury Field down the side of the river. Well Gordon Day's mother would stand outside her front door at the top of Queen Street and shout to Gordon that his dinner was ready, and we used to hear that.

   Biffy Charles and Frank Hancock were two of my friends, we'd go scrumping together and get chased. We'd bunk Biffy up the tree and he would stand in the tree and shake it until the apples fell off, then we would scramble and pick them up quick. There used to be a row over how many apples Biffy was going to have. We'd got it all worked out to a fine art. One night, it was a bit of a scramble; we went into Joe Randall's orchard and he was waiting there for us. That was a proper chase, fortunately he was a bit on the stout side and couldn't run as fast as us.

   Monday nights we used to play football in the High Street, along by the Black Lion, because there weren't many cars then. We'd put jackets down in the middle of the road for goal posts. 'Course Mondays was slaughtering day, so we used to go in Bigg's slaughterhouse and get these pigs' bladders and blow them up and use them for footballs. *George Turner*

Facing the Black Lion, there was a pond in front there. That hill used to come out of Church Road real steep. We used to get these old bicycles, no tyres on them, nothing like that, we made them up ourselves. We'd give each other a push, straight across the road and into the pond. *Biffy Charles*

There was four of us children in our family, that was one of the smallest families in the Avenue. Eight and nine was the usual, and Clark's there were 13 of them. I've seen 70 children playing in that square in the Avenue. *Albert Scott.*

As kids we used to tickle along with marbles in the gutter, flicking cigarette cards, and conkers. Of course in those days there wasn't

Fen End, now Astwick Road.

the traffic like there is today. The fastest thing that came through
Stotfold was the steam wagon from down Bowman's Mill. They
used it to cart stuff to their mill in Hitchin.

Down in Little London there was this stream, and as kids we
used to go there and get frog spawn and put it into jars. *Doug
Flitton*

I used to slide on the pond in winter. There was a very deep well in
the middle of the pond. My mother didn't like me going on there.
We used to get hold of each other's back and get in a long row and
keep sliding over, the ice used to break sometimes. *Phyllis King
neé Brown*

Before I left school I did a paper round for Jim Searle in the old
Post Office. I would go from Searle's at the top of the Avenue,
along Baldock Road down to Radwell, to the big houses there and
back along the footpath home; 1s 3d a week that's all I got. All I
had was a strap that they give me and I held these papers under
my arm. I used to walk, I didn't have a bike, I would run a lot of the
way. I loved it because I was out in the open.

When I lived at home I kept pigeons, I had about 30, this was on

The River at Fore Bridge, Stotfold.

Swimming in the river at the Ford Bridge.

the High Street, Swan Villas. We'd got a big shed down the bottom of the garden which dad let me use. I bought a bike, it was a James I think, cost about 10 quid, semi-racer. I'd take my pigeons out Sunday morning in a big basket on the back of my bike. I used to bike to Peterborough and let them go, they'd be home before I was. Sometimes I lost one. *George Shepherd*

We used to bend a twig down from a nice hedge and attach an old rotten potato on it and let it go, it used to fly up in the air quite nicely. We also made kites out of wallpaper, one time we had one flying for 24 hours, I thought that quite good.

Golden Corner was the place to have a nice swim, in fact, during the Feast week the Fair people came down there for a swim as well, but of course they didn't bother about costumes. We also swam in the river opposite the mill. Mr Randall used to let us nip in the mill and change there and then we'd run across the road and dive in from the bridge there. I'm afraid the river today is not as deep as it was then, it was over 8 feet deep then. *Claude Ingrey*

Chapter 3

The Daily Round

Living Conditions

Coping with everyday life in the old days was not always easy. Most people were poor; they worked long hours for small rewards. There were none of the modern conveniences available for the women of the family and many were 'tied to the kitchen sink' all day, every day. Families tended to be much larger, it was not uncommon to find a family of six or more children sharing a two-bedroom house. Despite these hardships, the general consensus of opinion was that life then was happier and more peaceful.

There was a certain pattern to life: Monday was wash day, Tuesday ironing day, Friday cleaning day and Sunday was a special day, reserved for church or chapel.

There was six of us in our family, four boys and two girls. When I was six we moved to Brook Street, there were some little old thatched cottages opposite the Stag, with just two bedrooms. It wasn't for the size of the house we moved but for the size of the garden. We all slept there somehow, we accepted that as a way of life. My father was a general labourer, he would put his hand to anything, building, land work, whatever came along. Makes you wonder how they did it, especially the women. My mum, she did mending, darning, sewing, cooking, all the washing was done by hand. And in the better weather I've known my mother to get up at four o'clock in the morning and walk about a mile to a pea field and do two or three hours pea picking. This village stood still for years and years, then in my lifetime things have changed, it changed as Letchworth grew. *Biffy Charles*

Our house like most others, depended on the wood-coal fire for all hot water, cooking and heating. Last thing at night, the hot cinders were put into the long-handled warming pan to warm the thick cotton sheets on the bed. The first job on rising would be to 'ruttle' the cinders left in the grate to remove the ashes which dropped into the ash pan underneath. This was then emptied on a heap in the garden for use on the path.

Below: Fen End, now Astwick Road, c. 1910.

Right: Chapel Yard, Rook Tree Lane

The paper and chopped firewood, which had been left all night on the iron-rack or shelf above the stove to ensure it was dry, would be stacked like a wigwam and the paper lit from a match from the box in a holder on the mantelpiece. The kettle would then be filled and when boiling would be removed to make the tea. Then a few lumps of precious coal would be added to the fire. The rate of burning was controlled by a 'damper' lever which altered the 'flue' hole and could divert the heat around the oven alongside. The amount of 'draft' was dependent on the chimney height and the direction of the wind. My mother would be able to judge the oven temperature by quickly opening the oven door to 'feel' the heat on her hand. We used a drop-down iron shelf which covered the front fire bars to heat the smoothing irons. To check if the iron was hot enough, Mum touched it lightly with a wet fingertip. If it made a sizzling noise, the iron was ready to use.

For wash days we had to light the little copper which was in the wash-house. To get the fire going we used sticks and old newspapers and all sorts of rubbish. The copper came in handy for other things – we used to make a very nice parsnip wine when parsnips were very plentiful. We also used the copper to boil our

Christmas puddings. If you got the fire going too much and you opened this wooden lid which covered the copper, you couldn't see across the wash-house for steam. You had to bale all the water out, there was no tap. *Claude Ingrey*

Mother had a copper, in a barn outside, and one of the old-fashioned iron mangles. There was only one tap between four cottages, you went outside and got your water and baled it in. She used to use the old 'blue bag' and it was all soda and sunlight soap, no washing powder. Mother used to take in washing too. My sister and I didn't think much of that because we used to have to take the washing back at nights before we went out with the boys or anything. We would have the washing basket between us and we'd take it up to Mrs Redhouse, because mother did her washing, and the washing for next door to Salisbury House, where a Mrs Lacey lived. *Florence Phillips née Gentle*

Most people had a well-scrubbed, deal-top table in the kitchen where we used to make rag rugs. People were very poor but always seemed to be happy. In this house of Grandma's down the Common, there used to be a big old cellar, Grandpa Dear used to keep a barrel of beer down there, and when different people used to come and see him on Sunday morning he used to fetch them a little drink out of the cellar. *Maud Castle née Seymour*

We used to go to bed with a candlestick – the risks we used to take! The table in the living room had a lovely cloth on it with little tassels all round and that had an oil lamp standing in the middle of it. And yet I never ever remember any child pulling that. The house would have gone up in flames. We had water outside, no bathroom, a toilet halfway up the garden, it was a bit primitive. *Lily Edmonds née Huckle*

Household Services

Life gradually became easier after the First World War, and the installation of sewers and electricity in the early '30s greatly improved living conditions. Up to then, people had relied on gas or paraffin to light their homes.

Gas

Prior to 1929 we had gaslight at home and when the mantle broke it was a tricky job to replace it. At our house we called in the local handyman to fix it. He took the new mantle from its box, fitted it onto the light, lit it with a match and it flared up. Afterwards the lightest touch would break it. Yet the glass globe had to be fitted over it. Even now I can hear Percy the handyman saying, 'Leave it to me Mrs Hyde, I can do it'. *Bert Hyde*

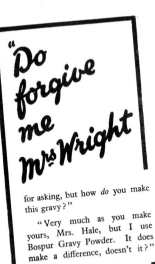

Waste disposal

There were no sewers – that was a lovely smell that was – you'd come walking home and you always knew somebody was emptying the bucket, they'd be digging a hole in the garden and it didn't 'alf pong. There were no street lights either. If you were running up the street and you couldn't hear one another's boot you would run into each other. You relied a lot on 'earing the old nails in the boots. *Biffy Charles*

Emma and Lila Seymour standing outside their home in Taylors Road.

When they were laying the sewer in the village and they'd got trenches in the road for laying the pipes, Freddy Hyde come out the Crown one night, straight in the trench. That was before the days of street lighting, like. Jim King said to him, 'What did you do that for?' 'Not for bloody swank', came the reply. *Sam Pooley*

There was a big upheaval when the sewers were put in. When it was first installed, my father, being very conservative, didn't have it laid on at the house straight away. We were fortunate at that time because we had a very large garden and there was no difficulty in disposing of the waste. *Doug Flitton*

Life was always pretty uneventful really. On bonfire night when they were laying the sewer, there was all these pipes laying around the village. Well, we'd got these little demons and kept chucking them up these pipes, they didn't 'alf bang. There were complaints flying everywhere. As it happened it was foggy that night and the coppers couldn't catch us. We'd all got pockets full of these little demons. *George Turner*

Electricity

When the electricity came to Stotfold they put the cables in, they used to have big reels. It's all underground in Stotfold, which they don't do now. There used to be 50 or 60 men with picks and shovels, the first one would take the top layer and the next one would take the next and so on, and by the time they got to the end it was deep enough for the cable, then they used to all get hold of the cable and start pulling. *Jack Brown*

We didn't used to have street lights, but as soon as you heard a person's footsteps you would know just who it was. In those days if you walked down Regent Street and fell off the path, you would break your neck because the path was so high. When the electricity started, it was all brought down by overhead cable, at that time from Letchworth. Ted Bew, he was an electrician, he still has relations in the village, he came to the front door to see my father about having electricity put in. My old dad was very conservative, he was a bit dubious and wanted to know all the ins and outs about the stuff. In the end he had three lights fitted, one in the hall, one in the landing up above and one in the room downstairs. Eventually I installed electricity in the rest of the rooms. When the cement and brick works at Arlesey started up it used to be such a load, it cut us off.

Eventually we did get a few street lights in Stotfold, although they were rather sparse. There used to be a switch box at the top of the Avenue and old Kelly had a key to unlock it. Every night at ten o'clock Kelly had to go, crutch and all, to open the box and pull the switch out so that all the street lights would go off. Old Kelly was marvellous the way he got round with his crutch, he used to ride a lady's bike. He also took round the old horse trolley with goods for Albert Brown. *Doug Flitton*

Food and Eating

At one time most people grew their own vegetables in the back garden and reared a few chickens there as well. Up until the late 20s many people also found room to keep a few pigs, and a common saying at the time was that you had to have £100 and a pig to live in Stotfold. The autumn was a particularly busy time in the kitchen and the smell of spices and fruit wafted around as preserves, jams and wines were made from the home-grown produce.

We used to grow all our own vegetables, there wasn't a weed about when Stan, my husband, was here. And he grew some lovely big apples; they were lovely and sweet, Blenheim Orange, I think. Stan liked his meat. He also liked cold vegetables and a bit of cheese with it. Or he'd just have cold greens with vinegar on. I've always been one to cook. I still do it. We used to cook the old-fashioned food and always had it at one o'clock and half-past four tea. My old boys laugh at me. *Mill Dear née Smith*

Bat-folding was popular with some folk. You had two pieces of shaped wood with a net stretched between, which would catch the birds. They used to put it over the hedge, scare the birds and trap them and they would use them for the oven. They would catch larks, sparrows, linnets. I sometimes cooked the birds. I had a moorhen once and that puzzled me, because you've got to skin them. *Doll Gentle née Peacock*

We used to go up to the hospital for basins of drippin'; because my aunt worked up there, we was allowed to go up there and get this drippin'. They used to call us what lived up Asylum Road, the 'asylum drips'. *Alf Cardell*

George and Wally Munt's mother used to kick the lot of them out every day at a certain time. She used to make what they called the Bedfordshire Clanger, a roly poly with jam at one end and meat at the other. *Doug Flitton*

We never did have much, but we always had good food coming out of the oven. When we used to rush home from school, there was

Two up, two down houses in Brook Street. Reg and Stan Trussell in the foreground.

always pies, spotted dicks, dumplings, lovely hot food. Mum used to cook on a range. She spent all her life looking after her children. *Olive Scott née Chambers*

When we lived down the Peewit we always had a pig hanging up on the wall, I used to cure it. We would just cut off a couple of slices when we needed it and put it straight into the pan. *Doll Howard née Westrope*

The 'Gentry'

Most towns and villages had a handful of families whose standard of living was above average. Some had inherited wealth, whereas others were self-made businessmen, but all kept a well-stocked larder and cellar with sufficient staff to ensure that everything ran smoothly on the domestic front.

Life at Salisbury House, Baldock Road

In the early 1900s, Salisbury House was occupied by Samuel Redhouse, the builder, and his family.

Salisbury House was a big house, we used to go there to Sunday lunch. I can see grandfather now, he was a marvellous man, very tall. Once, when he was in his old four-wheel gig he used to drive when he was older, he took me for a little ride and he went fast asleep. I was only a little boy and the old pony, 'Charley' took us along; frightened me to death. *Cecil Edwards*

He would never have meat on the table a second time, they used to have enormous joints of meat. What was left over went down to the village on the Monday morning.

They had maids in uniform, caps and aprons, always had a woman to clean. He had a boot boy to clean his boots and clean the knives. They used to roast the meat in front of the fire, on a spit. They made all their own bread. My Aunt Nancy, she always had in the pantry big boxes and tins full of cakes, and they had ginger beer in those bottles with the marble. I always wanted to get the marble out. That was such a treat.

Grandmother always wore a little black silk apron, a little cap with lace and bows and a long dress. She always used to wear a cap in the house, little caps made of lace with lavender bows in them. *Evelyn Blaker née Edwards*

Grandfather would often sit outside in the summer, he'd sit on this old chair. When the cherries were on the trees he used to rig up this bell in the tree which was attached to a long piece of string. Every time a bird came down to feast on the cherries, he'd pull this string and the bell would ring and scare it off. That fascinated me to death. *Cecil Edwards*

Mr and Mrs Samuel Redhouse in the garden of Salisbury House.

Life at Rook Tree House

Rook Tree Farm, which stood in Rook Tree Lane, was one of the six main farms of the village up to 1876. In that year the farmhouse in Rook Tree Lane was sold separately from the land. From about 1827 to 1876 the farm was worked by Mr Samuel Bowman, who was farming at the time of the 1830 Stotfold riots. One of his sons, Samuel jnr., farmed Bury Farm until about 1900. In 1857 two of his other sons went in business at Astwick mill, but only one, James, stayed there and carried on the milling business. James' youngest daughter married Mr Edward Smyth of Edworth, and when he became involved with the family business at Astwick mill he went to live in the old Bowman home (now Rook Tree House) in Rook Tree Lane which was convenient to Astwick. Mr and Mrs Smyth had two daughters, Ina and Joan.

The Bowmans had the house and farmed there, when they died it was let to somebody. Then, when father joined the mill, he and mother had to find somewhere near to live so they went there in 1906, I was born a year later. It was very derelict apparently. After we'd been there a while the ceiling fell down in the bedroom my parents were in. My father then had the place renovated. When this was happening, we went and lived at the vicarage for a year while the house was being altered. We had four-and-a-half acres of

Mr Samuel Bowman in foreground, standing in front of Rook Tree Farm which he worked from about 1827 to 1876.

The dovecote in the grounds of Rook Tree House.

land before the Government took some land as a compulsory purchase for the playing fields. There were stables, coach houses, and where the tennis court was, used to be the farmyard. The house had seven bedrooms, three receptions, there were beautiful old beams, and two staircases. When it was altered they turned the kitchen into the sitting room with a big bow window. And they altered upstairs because at one time you couldn't stand up in it. My room was new, that was over the brew house. That was where the brewers slept, years ago. *Joan Smyth*

They were travelling brewers who came once a year, a long time ago, and they would make the beer. They did it for all the farmers, because they also used to go where my father was born at Edworth. They would sleep a couple of nights and they always had a room over the brew house. The beer was for the farm workers. We used to pump up our water every day. In the courtyard, just outside the back door, there was an enormous well and at the back there was a little pump-house, and someone had to pump the water up every day to the tanks in the roof. *Ina Roberts neé Smyth*

Nanny came when I was born, she was 18. Her name was Annie Dilley from Astwick. She used to pinch my cheeks when we had visitors, so I looked healthy, it did hurt. She used to make us clean our teeth with primrose soap and soot. And do you know I've never liked cleaning my teeth ever since. She was a bit of a dragon, but we adored her. She worked for mother for many years. When we were older she used to come up on Saturday morning and do the vegetables for the weekend. She married Cooper our gardener and they lived down Little London. Then when he died she married a Castle. She had two children, Frank and Nancy. My sister used to collect cigarette cards and Frank used to bring the cards for Joan, but I had to pay him in kisses, behind the chestnut tree. *Ina Roberts neé Smyth*

We were very strictly brought up and used to have to work pretty hard. We had a dairy with slate shelves. The milk was kept in cans and I used to have to skim it twice a day. They were Jersey cows and the milk was terribly rich. I used to make the butter once a week. We used to sell that at Halls's. Churning was hard work.

If we had a tennis party, we had to make all the cakes and make the sandwiches and mark the lawn out, we also had to weed it by hand. We had to scrub the summer house out and scrub all the seats ready for the guests. We weren't supposed to read a book before the evening. We were never allowed comics on Sunday, only religious books. *Joan Smyth*

One day I had been very naughty and had been put in the corner by our governess, and old Brown, who was then our gardener, climbed the ladder to the nursery and said, 'I want her to help me

Rook Tree House c. 1907.

put the potatoes in, let her go'. So I was taken out of the corner to help plant the potatoes. We used to keep pigs, chicken, guinea fowl, ducks and geese. We had to help with the hay-making. We had little hay forks made by Eustace Ginn and little scythes. When Daddy came home from work he would go out and cut the nettles down and I had to go and cut nettles as well. The guinea fowl gave us beautiful eggs. Daddy had some lavender colour ones, they were very rare. Of course, they were very good to eat too and Daddy would give them away at Christmas. *Ina Roberts neé Smyth*

I used to dislike it very much in the spring because when the guinea fowl hatched out we had to teach them to go in at night, otherwise they would go up in the trees and then we wouldn't be able to catch them for Christmas. So we were dragooned to train the guinea fowl and that took quite a long time. I never did like the spring-time much. At one time we used to keep goats for milk, because I wasn't supposed to have cow's milk for some reason or other. And I used to have to go and feed them after lunch. One day the billy goat knocked me down and tossed me, I was about two or three. I've never liked horned things since. *Joan Smyth*

We also used to keep Dexter cows, they were black and quite small, they gave a lot of milk. One went mental when it had its first

Opposite, above left: Ina Smyth in her wicker pram, 1911.

Opposite, above right: Annie Dilley, nanny, holding Ina with Joan Smyth standing at her side, 1911.

Opposite below: Rook Tree House c. 1910.

Above: Mrs Smyth and family members in the horse and trap.

Left: Cooper the gardener (Annie Dilley's husband) with Bertha the Dexter cow, 1910.

calf. Daddy was pumping water in the field opposite Rook Tree and I was playing in the field and suddenly this Dexter charged. I can hear Daddy now, he said, 'Stand up to it'. Well I wasn't standing up to it, I ran and stood behind Daddy. We had to have it put down in the end.

We had to learn how to milk the cows in case we had to in an emergency. For six months we had to do our stint of getting up in the morning at six o'clock. I loved milking the cows but Joan didn't. I would collect the milk in my seaside pail and then would give it to the cats, we always had cats. We also kept doves in the dovecote. There were nesting boxes from the first floor right up to the top. We used to keep tumblers and fantails. We also used to keep rabbits in a shed in cages, I think there were four bucks and I don't know how many rabbits, different breeds. One day Daddy was going out for the day and he put me in charge of the rabbits. I had to feed them and see they had water and clean them out. I felt so sorry for them that I let them all out together. When Daddy came home he wasn't very pleased with my efforts. Daddy used to sell the pelts for gloves, just as I used to catch moles for the pelts during the First World War. The only thing I had against Daddy was that he used to make me give half the money to my sister. I used to dry them and cure them and then send them to some place, I think I got 6d a pelt, which was a lot of money. I used to catch them in traps, they're very easy to kill. I used to do the skinning. I really thought it unfair that my sister got half the money.

We had to catch white butterflies, I think we got a farthing a hundred or perhaps it was a penny. Joan didn't like killing them, I didn't mind that. She used to put her foot on them, so Daddy couldn't count them and she didn't always get her money if they were too squashed.

Mother used to drive a trap, she used to go everywhere in it. Granny Bowman – she was an agnostic – she was very modern. We used to wear boots and she said to mother one day, she must have been about 85, 'It's quite time those children were taken out of boots and were allowed to wear shoes'. She got us all the modern things.

Mrs Johnny Pateman, she taught me to read, I went there every day. Joan went to Woking and then we both went to Bedford to a private school, we were boarders.

Father used to take lots of photographs, he had a box camera with half plates then he changed to a quarter plate one. I used to help him on Sundays. We used to do all the developing and printing, everything. We used to rush out with the frames and put them in the garden in the sun and we would keep looking at them to see if they had 'cooked' enough. Daddy had a darkroom with a red window to it. He was a very versatile person. *Ina Roberts née Smyth*

Stotfold House

Stotfold House, also known as Cross Roads Villa, was the largest house in Stotfold. Built in 1866 on 234 acres of land, it had 20 rooms plus stables, a courtyard and vegetable garden. Cricket and football were played on the meadow land belonging to the house. John Ray, the builder, the Blaker family and Cook family had all owned or occupied it at various times.

I lived in Stotfold House for about 12 months in the early 20s. The house had a very nice entrance with a circular drive, and enormous lawns. There was a summer-house which my daughter used to go in and pretend she was Mrs. Tittlemouse. There were no end of strawberries growing there, and there were fruit trees in the kitchen garden. We also had a tennis court which was in the paddock just off the side of the house. *Evelyn Blaker née Edwards*

Women in service

Prior to the opening of the factories in Letchworth and Baldock, the only employment available to young women was in service. In many cases this meant leaving Stotfold and their families.

I was in service most of the time. I worked for Miss Meskimmon first, but she said I should do something better. I never stayed anywhere more that 12 months. I went to the Node at Codicote, and I would cycle home now and again on a Sunday. I would ride back and put my bike away in the shed. You had to be in by ten o'clock, you mustn't be a minute late. The gardeners locked the door and one night they locked the door before ten and I couldn't get in. So I put my bike near the gate, climbed on and over I went that way. I went to the gardener and grumbled about it and as we was walking back the clock struck ten.

I really enjoyed my time in service. I also worked for the Queen Mother before she became Queen at 145 Piccadilly. *Emily Cardell née Millard*

My first job after I left school, about 1914, was helping Bessie Smith's mother. Bessie was due to be born so they asked me if I would take the others out. Mrs Smith had a trained nurse, and a woman from Shefford to do the cooking, well she couldn't cook anything. Fancy me, younger than her, knowing more about cooking. *Mill Dear née Smith*

My mum left school in the morning and in the afternoon she went straight down Kitchiner's, at Astwick and stayed there for 55 years. She brought all them Kitchiner boys up. She first of all went there as a nursemaid, then she carried on as a nanny for the six children. When she first went there, George and Frank had just started boarding school, but the others was all there. There was Rupert, Peter, Doug and Colin. She left there to get married at Astwick Church and then ended up going back again. I used to have to go down there with her on the back of her bike. Because my mum worked down the farm we used to eat quite well. Sometimes she would bring a pheasant home, or a partridge, or a rabbit. *Peg Humphries née Millard*

In about 1920 I went to work for the Redhouses at Salisbury House, Stan and Hilary lived there then. I only used to go from nine until two, and I had my dinner which was lovely. I earnt five shillings a week. When Hilary got married they had this great big marquee in the garden. *Florence Phillips née Gentle*

My sister was in service at Redhouse's; she used to work for Stan's mum, and there was another old lady who lived with her. They treated my sister very well, there were no complaints there. She was more or less accepted as one of the family. She did her work and had the run of the house. They were quite a wealthy family, well respected. I've got no complaint with none of what we call the big families we had then. There was the Smith family down Regent Street, Whiteheads, another gentleman, the Brownings. They would always go out of their way to help a person, but if anybody crossed them that was another story. But you could live with them. *Biffy Charles*

We had domestic help, and I remember one time we employed a lady who had been recommended through a domestic agency in Hitchin. Unfortunately she didn't last long because one evening she came back from the pub, rather the worse for wear, she had a bottle in each pocket. She was so tipsy she couldn't get up the step and we had to put her to bed. My husband was not very pleased, and the next day she was asked to pack her bags. He took her to Hitchin market place and just left her there. *Odette Kitchiner née Randall*

Familiar names

Some families have lived in Stotfold a long time. There are Millards still living in the village nearly 400 years after the first was mentioned in 1609. Other surnames which crop up through the years are Brown, Dear, Howard, Hyde and Gentle, and at one time it was said that if you knew the surnames you could tell which chapel each family attended. It was acknowledged that the Browns went to the Salvation Army, the Dears to the Wesleyan Chapel, the Howards to the Primitive Methodist in Brook Street and the Hydes to the Old Baptist Chapel.

Nicknames

Why were there so many nicknames in a small village? The theory is that because there were so many people who shared the same surname, it was much easier to use a nickname, thus eliminating all confusion. Quite often that nickname would be passed down from father to son. It is strange, though that very few women were given nicknames.

Above: Tinny Triplow.

Below: Black Lion outing, c. 1949.

Nicknames were usually given in a friendly and light-hearted manner as these examples of local names show.

Below: Spiffer Gadsden behind the bar at The Chequers.

Bottom: Nigger.

Banger	Hard Hat	Ox Legs	Sidgel
Biffy	Knuckles	Packy	Skinny Jack
Blacky	Little Hat	Paggy	Smarty
Blowsey	Long Clara	Panel	Smick
Bonus	Long Jack	Pangle	Snowball
Bricky	Long Sid	Parry	Spiffer
Bungy	Merry Widda'	Pickle	Squint
Bunny	Merryheart	Pip	Sticker-sole
Bushel	Minna	Poke	Stygy
Buttons	Modgy	Porky	Swaffer
Chelsea	Moment	Pudder	Tank
Chubby	Mooner	Puff	Tinny
Chuck	Mossy	Puggy	Tinware
Connor	Mouldy	Pummer	Tom-Tit
Cozzy	Muggins	Puppy	Toot
Curly	Musso	Quack	Treader
Dicker	News of the	Sarcy	Wes'on
Dubby	World	Schemer	Wupper
Duke	Nigger	Scummer	Yinky
Eggneck	Ninna	Shakel	Yokker
Freddy Wonk	Nobby	Shirty	Yorky
Hanky	Notty	Sidgy	Zoot

This happened somewhere on the Grange farm in the time of Charley Vaughan, around 1870. One of the Porter family, named Caleb, was helping with the harvest when a hare ran out of the corn and sped past the spot where the men were standing. Caleb exclaimed, 'Yink my leg Mr Vaughan, if it had not been for my yinking leg I would have caught that 'are'. So they nicknamed him Yinky, and ever afterwards the oldest son was always known as Yinky Porter, and it was so in my day. *Albert Scott*

Characters

My grandfather Howard lived up behind the old Post Office on the High Street, he was courting my grandma and she lived down this way. Well, he was going home one night and this figure walked by the side of him as he was going by Tythe Cottage. He kept walking and kept looking at it and then said, 'Oh well, mate, I think I'll have me old pipe'. As he lit his match to his pipe, it just vanished. He told us that no end of times. *Peg Humphries née Millard*

Sarcy Hyde lived in St Olives, and when I was a boy and lived in Arlesey Road I used to go down the garden and stand where he was, and he would be ploughing the ground at the back of St Olives. He bought all these horses from the First World War, they'd all got a broad arrow on them. I was fascinated by horses when I was little. I used to be about with him, and he used to say to me, 'Come in the office I'll pay you your money'. He gave me thruppence and a bunch of turnips.

He used to have what we called Wembley, it was a medda' up Hitchin Road. He used to go to all the sales and buy up all the farm stuff up. Then he would bring it back and stand it all in the medda'. He used to take me down there with him, I was only three or four years old. He would say to me, 'Bruce Pateman would like these, wouldn't he?' They were bullock pans for putting food in, he'd got them all standing there. They called it Wembley because of the junk. *Albert Scott*

Dubby Day used to live in Common Road and he was a town crier, he used to go round with his bell and announce the council meetings which were held in the Tin Box. *Jack Brown*

Drummer Gentle was a character, we used to lend him our horse for cutting some corn near the cemetery. I had this queer old bike I'd made up out of an old lady's bike, it had a 26-inch wheel in a 28-inch frame and no brakes. Anyway Drummer wanted to get to the Chequers for a quick pint, so he said, 'I'll borrow your bike, boy'. I told him that it had got no brakes. 'I'll be alright.' Before I could tell him that the handlebars used to twist if you got in a rut, he was in the ditch. *Claude Ingrey*

Deany was a character, he was walking his dog one night and somebody said, 'The dog's getting old'. 'Yeah', he said, 'it's getting so the lampposts are too far apart for him'. *Sam Pooley*

Long Clara always used to come out of her cottage and empty her teapot against the building. Her daughter Becky, she upset me one day coming home from school and I called *her* Long Clara. Well Long Clara came up to mother and said, 'Becky was a young lady and wasn't to be called Long Clara'. So mother said, 'My son's a young man and your Becky ain't no angel'. The reason they called her Long Clara was that she was such a tall woman. *Jack Brown*

Opposite where I lived at the top of Queen Street were two little cottages, old Granny Keats used to live in one. She was a miserable woman and we used to think she was an old witch. One day, another young girl and myself, we were very naughty, we threw some mud on her door. In those days you were very frightened of your teacher, you always did what they told you. Someone told teacher who it was, and we were sent with a pail and water and had to wash the mud away. *Florence Phillips née Gentle*

Granny Keats was the oldest person I can remember, she used to scare me. We had to go through the churchyard to the Girls' School. She used to roam around there. She had one of these old-

Above: Snowball.
Below: Deany

ETONBURY.
ARLESEY.
Nr. HITCHIN.

Quarter Ending *Mar 31st* 1924

Mr Willsher

1 The Avenue

To Dr. W. W. MacNaught.

£   s.   d.

For Professional Services   ·   :   :

a/c Rendered   1 – 13 – 0

Bill for professional services from Dr W W MacNaught, 1924.

fashioned black hooded cloaks. I can't ever remember seeing her face because of this hood, she was frightening to look at.

They said that when Skinny Jack died they had to cut his boots off, because he'd never taken them off. He used to have a 'gammy' foot that he dragged along. *John Cramp*

The football ground used to be rented by Bruce Pateman in them early days, he gave Skinny Jack permission to put his caravan there. He used to do a little bit for Bruce up at the slaughter house, a bit of clearing up. They used to put stones down his chimney. If I remember rightly, I think the caravan that he had, I'm almost certain this is so, was old Mrs Reynolds, what used to do the sweets. When she died he bought the caravan and moved it from Common Road to Little London. *Reg Saunders*

Essential services

Other very important aspects of village life were the services provided by the doctors and nurses, fire brigade and police.

Doctors and nurses

Up until 1933, Stotfold had no doctor in residence in the village. If anybody needed medical attention the doctor had to come all the way from Arlesey. Prior to the National Health Act of 1946 all doctors' bills had to be paid by the individual, hence doctors were only called out in dire circumstances.

The Hospital Fund was established in the village to help with the cost of hospital treatment, money being raised by various means: individual donations, Hospital Day (see page 144), socials and concerts.

The Stotfold and Astwick Nursing Association was formed in about 1919 to help with administering to the sick and delivering babies and continued up until 1949.

Dr Heptinstall

Dr 'Ep'install, one day when I was ill bought me a dove, I never did know what made him bring it to me, lovely bird it was. He was a nice old gentleman. He used to have a man drive him round in a horse and cart. He lived in the same house as Farmer. *Alf Cardell*

One day this fella Joe Payne had a stomach ache so he went to see Dr 'Ep'install. He asked for some medicine for his bad stomach. The doctor mixed him some up and gave him the bottle and charged sixpence, and tuppence back for returning the bottle. So he took the cork out and drunk it right back and said, 'There y'are, I'll pay you fourpence'. The doctor said, 'If I'd known you were going to do that I'd have put something different in it'. *Albert Scott*

Nurse Bishop

When my little half-brother was born, we were living in Regent Street at the time. Nurse Bishop had a caravan behind one of the shops, and she asked me if I would go and get her black bag from her caravan. So my sister and I went up there, the caravan was unlocked and we went in and got this bag. I was dying to open it because I was certain the baby was in it, and I did want to see that, but I didn't. The temptation was nearly too much. *Lily Edmonds neé Huckle*

The Fire Brigade

Stotfold Fire Brigade, the first place they had was by the side of Johnny Pateman's shop, then they moved it down to the Tin Box. They had a hand truck. One day they reckon there was a fire up Whip Jacks and they got the truck out to take up there. On their way there Aubrey Castle called out, 'Where's the fire?' So they stopped to tell him where the fire was and in so doing they tipped the truck up. *Albert Scott*

The fire station used to be in Regent Street opposite Church Road, there was a fire bell there. My grandad was a member of the fire service. One day there was a fire down the Common, it was caused by tarring, it was that thick it had caught light. Grandad went down on his bike ahead of the fire truck and he got flour from somebody and chucked this on the fire and put it out. *Bert Gentle*

Garden's Bakery Fire, High Street, 1908. The bakery was completely rebuilt after the fire.

Members of Stotfold Fire Brigade.

My brother got half-a-crown for ringing the bell once when there was a fire up the Conservative Club. Yinky Porter and Stan Rollin's older brother was in the fire brigade. They could never put a fire out because it was an old hand pump. *Sam Pooley*

When John Ray, the builder, lived at Stotfold House, the electric organ caught fire. At that time the fire station was a little hut next to the Tin Box. The fire bell rang and they were called out. There was 'Pangle', Jamie Ball, Frank Peacock and one other. They couldn't find the key. We lived in the bungalow which was nearby and my brother was hanging out of the window, he'd got pleurisy at the time and there was about four inches of snow on the ground. They were calling each other everything, they went and borrowed a pole axe to try and get the door open. Well, by the time they'd got there, Letchworth Fire Brigade had been and put the fire out. *Jack Brown*

The Police

There wasn't much crime in the villages and the local policeman was mainly concerned with small offences. People never felt the need to lock their doors, nor did they worry if they were out late at night.

Turland was the policeman here for many years, that was a while back, he lived down the Avenue. That was when wireless first came in and he had a big pole in the garden. We used to get through the hedge and shake the copper's pole and that would upset the reception. Of course that tickled us, to do that to a policeman and to get away up the road without being caught. We shook Turland's pole quite often. *Biffy Charles*

I think Busby was the first policeman in Stotfold, then there was Toleman and Smith. Smithy was always pinching Jingle for something. Him and his brother used to go round digging dandelion roots and wild rhubarb and sell them. At the time, in the field opposite the Two Chimneys, they used to have grass track meetings in there. We were outside Phil Howard's billiard hall one day and Jingle was tearing round on his bike. He was telling us about this chap who had been racing, and he was tearing round on his bike trying to imitate this bloke and as he swung round, his front wheel went straight through PC Smith's legs. Smithy pinched him for riding dangerously on a bike. Anyhow, we was up the High Street several days afterwards, in what was then the Post Office, and Smithy comes walking up Brook Street and shouts out, 'Jingle, I want you'. 'Ah, Mr Smith, I suppose you've got a summons for me.' 'To tell you the truth, Jingle, I've got two.' Jingle lived down Brook Street, just before the Pig and Whistle. We would go and sit there and play cards sometimes, and when we left we had to leave the money for the electric on the shelf. *George Turner*

Crimes

Over the years Stotfold has had its scandals and murders. The Stotfold riots of 1830 (see page 12) obviously caused quite a stir for it to be widely reported in the national press.

In August 1943, a nurse was murdered at the Three Counties Hospital. PC Fisher arrested Reginald Rowley, who was subsequently charged with the murder.

Perhaps the most infamous crime was the cigarette robbery in August 1948. Over a million cigarettes were stolen from a bonded warehouse in Dover. Two people living in Stotfold at the time were prosecuted for receiving nearly half a million of the cigarettes, both were given prison sentences.

The most talked about crime was that of Dick Bew stealing a horse. It was amusing to hear all the different stories related to the same crime. Dick Bew did steal a horse, that is fact, but which story is true?

Dick Bew stole an 'orse, nothing was too heavy for Dick, if you wanted a steam roller he would get you one. He nicked this 'orse out of the medda' and he was walking it to a market, well up the road, Peterborough or somewhere like that, to some 'orse fair. He got picked up, poor old chap, he was a devil. *Biffy Charles*

Dick Bew stole this 'orse. The policeman here at the time was Godman, and he traced this horse up Mill Path and he followed it and reckoned it went to Cambridge and followed it up. He went in

PC Smith, 1938.

this stable where this 'orse was and took Teddy Castle with him, who owned the 'orse. When Teddy Castle went into the stable and talked to the 'orse, and it neighed and knew him. Dick Bew got six months for that. *Albert Scott*

Old Dick Bew, he went to prison several times. He stole a horse once, it belonged to a chap named Castle who lived up Baldock Road. He took it to St Ives market and sold it. Dick used to be a drover, he knew all the highways and byways. He would never go along the main roads. When he went to St Ives, there was a certain amount of police activity going on, they didn't see him, but he saw them. So he came to a field and he backed the horse backwards across this field so if the police saw the hoof marks they would think he was going the other way. If he'd had sense enough to burn his trousers they wouldn't have caught him. But the police went to his house and he'd got his trousers in a bath of water trying to wash the hairs out. So even that at time, they would compare the hairs on his trousers with the horse's hairs. 'Course he was done.

He'd keep greyhounds, and do a lot of poaching. He'd sit in the White Horse with his greyhound and he would take half crown bets that he would leave the White Horse with his dog and be back within half-an-hour with a hare. He always won his bet.

He also used to take bets when they used to cut the corn by hand using a scythe. At that time they would think nothing of walking to Royston or anywhere like that, and sit in a pub where they weren't so well known. He would take bets that he could cut an acre of corn in an hour with a scythe. Of course they used to say it couldn't be done. He'd take no end of bets and he would go out and do it.

One time Dick Bew got caught by a Henlow policeman doing something or other. He got summonsed and fined. Some time later he went over to Henlow when he knew the policeman would be away on duty, like. He went into his back garden and picked all his peas. He came home, shelled all the peas and put the peas in a shoe box and took them down the Post Office and posted them back to him. *George Turner*

Chapter 4

Going Shopping

Established in 1840, Ebsworth's, at the bottom of the Crofts, was the first shop in Stotfold. It was an off licence and post office as well as a grocer's and draper's. When he stopped trading in around 1906, the post office business was transferred from Ebsworth to Jim Searle in the High Street, now Fourboys. Three of Ebsworth's assistants, Charlie Levitt, Jim Pateman and Johnny Pateman then started up on their own account, Charlie Levitt being his official successor. He traded from the building which is now the Co-op, and, when he stopped trading, his assistant, Louie Brown, started up on her own on The Green. William Bigg, the butcher at the Black Lion was in business by 1869, and William Smith, dealer in all kinds of new and second-hand furniture as well as being a general dealer, was on the scene by 1894, in Regent Street, now Palmer's. This was to become Stotfold's biggest shop. This chapter includes just a few of the shops that were around in the first half of this century.

Ebsworth's, 3 The Crofts

As far as I know, Ebsworth's was the first shop in Stotfold. It was a general store down the Crofts, next door to where Dave Chellew now lives. Mr Levitt had the shop after Ebsworth. It must have been about 1955-ish when there had been a thunderstorm and my cousin and I went down the field to pick up some timber. The sun came out and the slates were all wet and that had got 'Ebsworth' written on the slates right across the roof. During the Boer War, the telegraph used to come down there to say who had been killed. Up the top of the Crofts there used to be a 'snob'* who had a racing bike, F Hyde. He lived in Bigg's Row, as they used to call it, and he had a little place built on the end of the wash houses as his 'snobs' workshop. The wall on the end of the workshop had got 'F Hyde' in red brick. Anyway, when the telegrams used to come to say who had been killed, the man down Ebsworth's shop used to whistle and Mr Hyde would come out with his racing bike, charge down the Crofts, pick up the telegram and deliver it. Now my uncle Vince could whistle the same as the fella from the shop, and when

Your Soles need attention !
GO TO
CHURCH,
62, THE AVENUE, STOTFOLD.
Boot and Shoe Repairs neatly and quickly executed.
Hand sewn work a speciality.

W. G. KING,
48, The Green, Stotfold,
for
High-Class Groceries, Fruit, Confectionery, Tobacco, Cigarettes, &c.
Lyons' Cakes, Pastries, &c., a speciality.

W. COOK,
HIGH STREET, STOTFOLD.
Groceries, Provisions, Confectionery. Tobacco.
PATENT MEDICINES.
Cheapest Possible Prices. Visit also our Green-grocery Department.

1   *Shoemaker or mender.

they were old boys he used to whistle and Mr Hyde would come tearing out on his bike only to find that there was no telegram. That happened until he got a slap on the head. *David Shepherd*

The majority of people didn't get paid until Saturday and they always did their shopping Saturday afternoon or evening. Ebsworth's used to be so busy, so to try and get people to come later, any lady that went after ten o'clock on Saturday night to get her groceries was rewarded with a glass of stout. *George Turner*

Messrs W Smith & Sons, Regent Street

My father and grandfather used to go with the horse and trolley to London to the sale rooms and go and fetch a load of furniture, it was second-hand in those days. My grandfather always said that he would give a £100 for them to fill in Wilbury Hill, because by the time they got back from London the horses were very tired.

They used to set to and wash and scrub it all down and Wilfred Smith, no relation, used to polish and do it all up in our workshop at 68 Regent Street. He started with the firm when my mother and father came back from their honeymoon. There also used to be the removal lorries and they used to have the marquees, which they put up all over everywhere. When I was about eight I went to the Priory at Hitchin, they used to put a big marquee up there. I helped pull the rope up, it was such a long one. *Bessie Upchurch née Smith*

This tale goes back to when Ernie Smith was running the shop. Turby Gentle used to have an account there. He was always sending his men down there if they wanted any little odds and ends, screws and nails. He bowls in Ernie's shop one day, I was in there at the time. Ernie said, 'Just the gentleman I want to see, I keep wondering about your account, I've been sending you a bill regular for six months'. Turby said, 'I can't understand that, I've seen no bill,' eggin' Ernie on. Turby never paid nobody unless he was forced to. Turby said, 'Now then, how did you send it?' 'By post', said Ernie. 'Now what stamp did you put on, was it a ha'penny stamp or a three ha'penny stamp?' 'Well,' Ernie said, 'Same as all bills, ha'penny stamp.' 'Aarh,' said Turby, 'that's where you done wrong, I never open those with a ha'penny stamp on'. *George Turner*

We always went up Smith's and rigged ourselves out with second hand carpets. He always saved the second-hand carpets for the travellers at Stotfold Feast time. Thems that wanted it always got their carpets from Smith's. *Doll Howard née Westrop*

Frank Smith used to be a piano tuner, and they employed the man with a white wes'cot (Wilfred Smith) who did the furniture repairs and french polishing, and then after that, when radio come, out

W Smith & Sons, removal van.

W. SMITH & SONS,
STOTFOLD, Beds.

We beg to announce that we are arranging an

EXTENSIVE WIRELESS EXHIBITION
during *SEPTEMBER, FOR ONE WEEK.*

The full range of Receivers of the following Manufacturers
will be displayed

**MARCONI,   PYE,   COSSOR,   PHILLIPS,
ULTRA,   FERRANTI,   ECKO,   ALBA,
G.E.C.,   MCMICHAEL,   TELSON.**

Admission Free.   Watch for OPENING DATE.

Harold used to repair radios and sell dry batteries and recharge your accumulator every week. *Jack Brown*

When Bessie Smith used to have what is now Palmer's newsagent's that used to be an ironmongers, you could buy everything from a carpet, to a wardrobe, to a pin, to a nut, to a bolt, to a pair of scissors, everything, and Bessie would tear up and down that shop and know where everything was. *Hilary Saunders neé Devereux*

W Bigg Butcher, High Street

My father's butcher shop was at the side of the Black Lion, we also had the slaughterhouse at the back. We had to carry the meat in from the slaughterhouse and hang it up. And at Christmas-time, we used to have them all displayed in the front. *John Bigg*

The Biggs were a lovely family, I couldn't speak high enough of them. Will Bigg was noted for his brawn, he could make brawn. *Biffy Charles*

We used to take a basin up to Bigg's, he made faggots which were cooked at Keeper's and they used to come back on this old hand trolley in a metal basin. Mr Bigg would push these from Keeper's, they weren't covered up. We'd wait for two faggots for between six of us and we'd say, 'Mum says, please can she have some gravy with the faggots'. *Edward Bowskill*

When we was boys, John Bigg used to get hold of us when we come out of school to pull the bullocks up. He used to put a rope round the bullock and pull it up to get its head on the block, and he used to knock it down with a pole axe, and make a hole in its brain. We used to stand and watch it and didn't think anything about it. I helped Bill Randall ever so many times, they used to lay a sheep on the rack and make a hole behind its ear to get the blood out of it. *Albert Scott*

Sometime during the 1920's, when I was about ten, there was a big epidemic of foot and mouth disease in Stotfold. All the men turned out and all the animals were killed at Bigg's and they were brought down in this field, and there were big pits dug. This was where Roecroft school is now. The men had to dip their feet in disinfectant, but us kids had to stand at the top, out of the way. My father helped to bury the animals. We even went to watch the animals be killed. This was in a shed at the back of the Black Lion. And they used lime on the carcasses. *Florence Phillips née Gentle*

Next to the old garage opposite the Black Lion, we used to have a big shed in the back there where we made pork pies, we would sell them to the local shops. *John Bigg*

I learnt the pie trade at Bigg's and they gave me a lovely reference when I left. We used to make the pies, lovely they were, thruppence each. Christmas-time, they had a 50-gallon copper and they would shove these gammon hams in, then they would put the bread crumbs on them and use a piece of greaseproof paper to make a sort of flower. Most of the hams were cooked for special orders. *Biffy Charles*

One day old Mr Bigg got me and my brother Fred to go over there to catch some rats, because there was a lot of them about. This was on a Saturday we bought a tin of carbide, it's solid stuff. We went over there and put some down the 'oles, then put some water on it and it gives off a gas. We caught 37 rats using this stuff. *George Shepherd*

J Pateman, Butcher, Regent Street

Pateman had a butcher's shop in Regent Street where Beale's is now. I remember going to the butcher's for Mum for sixpenneth of pudding beef, and he'd give you the beef and always put your suet in as well, that was free. *Lily Edmonds née Huckle*

When Jim Pateman died, his shop was taken over by his son, George, Bruce's brother. Times were bad and many people got into debt. George felt it was time he took some action over his own bad payers. So he placed a notice in the window of the shop saying that people would be advised to settle their arrears as he intended to put up a list of the names of the debtors the next week. He finished up by writing that people were 'garsping' to see the names. *Claude Ingrey*

E J Pateman, Grocer, Regent Street

I spent a lot of time with Johnny Pateman; I served behind the counter there. I was only about five or six, but I was allowed to serve. *Ina Roberts née Smyth*

J. PATEMAN,
FAMILY BUTCHER,
STOTFOLD.
Familes waited upon daily.
Beef, Pork, Mutton, Poultry, and Sausages.

Dark Lane, now Church Road. In foreground Mr and Mrs Jim Pateman, and son George with the cattle, c. 1928.

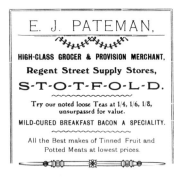

I used to take Johnny Pateman's empties back down to the Chequers, and get the money back on the bottles. He used to give me tuppence for doing that and, of course, bringing the full one back. I had a wicker basket with handles. When you went in the shop there was this big long counter on the right, but I can't remember what was on the left. I can see him now – he'd fill the bags up, especially the sugar bags and he'd bonk, bonk them on the counter, then fold the bag over and over. *John Cramp*

Crawley's, Regent Street

In those days it was a shop chiefly to do with outfitting, furnishing and footwear. My father married one of the Crawley daughters. My grandfather, John Crawley, owned a shop in Mill Street, Bedford, chiefly to do with footwear, and they had this one which my father, Cyrus, managed. At the back was a repair shop and a man named Bill King, was a regular 'snob' as they used to call a boot repairer in those days. Old Frank Cooper, who had an iron on his foot was another one, he also used to do weddings and funerals with a horse and carriage. He would put his top hat on. My father used to go round to the surrounding villages, Stamford, Southill, Broom and those types of places. In those days it wasn't footwear like it is today, flimsy light shoes, they were real heavy hob-nail boots. Frank would go round with the van and collect up nearly a van load of farm labourers' boots to be repaired.

My father also did gent's outfitting. In those days you could have a thundering good three-piece suit made-to-measure, for a fiver. Shoes were about half-a-crown a pair, five bob was a real tip-top pair. Kiddies' shoes were about sixpence a pair.

On the furniture side, not only did he sell the furniture, he also used to repair it, if the webbing or springs went. He would collect the chairs from the customer and bring them in, and he used the hop sacks from my uncle's brewery for putting on the bottom of the chair before the webbing or springs were added, it was very strong.

There used to be a roundsman called Snuggs, who worked for my father – Mrs King at Broom is his daughter. Frank Charles, Caleb's son, used to work for my father and went round with Snuggs. They used to go out with a little pony and trap.

My father also used to supply paraffin oil, the storage tanks were kept up the yard. I went up there one day and opened the tank, shut the door and then walked away. Before very long it all came pouring out onto the road like a river. Somebody spotted it and quickly turned it off, but a few gallons had been lost by then. My dad said, 'Who did it?' I was scared stiff and didn't own up, but he knew who it was. That was the only time that my father gave me the stick. Father insisted if I had told the truth he would not have caned me, he said, 'Liars and thieves, they're no good to anybody'. *Doug Flitton*

Mr and Mrs Charles outside the fish shop in Common Road, c. 1925.

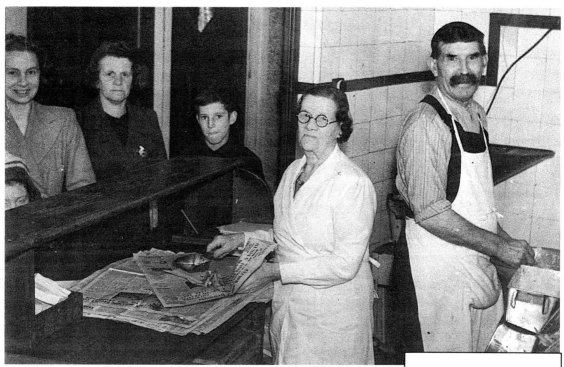

C J Charles, Fish Shop, Common Road

The reason my grandfather, Caleb, went into the business was that he was a smallholder who couldn't sell all his potatoes, so he decided to put them to good used in this way. His first shop was in a little corrugated building down Common Road, which he took over from Hubert Taylor some time after 1924. The pans of oil were like open coppers. In the old days they used to buy what they called a 'kit' of fish, it was like a wicker basket, a mixed 'kit' was 7s 6d and that was sent all the way from Grimsby by train. My father used to go on his push bike to Arlesey and would put it on the front and cycle home, and my grandfather would stand there ready because as my dad got off, the bike tipped up. *Barbara Bowskill née Talbot*

There used to be two fish shops, one was down Queen Street and the other was down Common Road in a little tin hut. I used to buy an ha'p'eth of crittlin's, they were the residue bits of hardened fat, but we used to think it was great to get a ha'p'eth of crittlin's from Mr Charles. *Claude Ingrey*

Above: Mr and Mrs Charles in the fish shop in Regent Street, c. 1945.

Dick Strike (Richard Smith), Brook Street

There were two forms in Dick Smith's shop and we used to sit in there. One of us would get up and ask him for a ha'p'eth of sweets.

Dear's Cycle Shop, Arlesey Road, Doris and Gladys Dear standing outside, c. 1913.

He'd serve him and then sit down again, then the next one would ask him for ha'p'eth of sweets, so up he'd get again. We'd be in there for an hour or more and he hadn't done a stroke of work. One of these nights John Bigg was in there, and when he got up to get his sweets, he'd got a stink bomb which he smashed on his 'obbin' foot. Dick come back, smells it and lights this brown paper to stop the smell, and promptly turned us all out. *Alf Cardell*

Dick Strike used to sell fireworks, he'd have them set out on the table. Five or six of us would go in there together, get him in such a state he wouldn't know where he was. We used to pinch more than we bought. Freddy Trussell let a firework off one night, and it went off with quite a bang. He said, 'Well that didn't go bad for a pinched 'un'. *Sam Pooley*

Albert Brown, Grocer, Brook Street

Albert Brown rented this shop in Brook Street from Jim Woodhouse's mum, and then, when the lease come up, Jim Woodhouse had it. Albert did his business from there, but he didn't live there. He lived along Baldock Road. Albert had a greengrocery and he sold all oddments, tin stuff, anything really where he could get a bob or two. He had his stuff all in the winda' and all inside in sacks and boxes. He used to fetch me out of school to do a bit of 'orse sowing – he had some ground along Arlesey Road, near the gas 'ouse. Then he decided to start a round in Letchworth, so he asked me to come as his boy, running round the 'ouses, Saturdays only. He'd take a trolley with 'orse. Kelly did it for 'im as well. There were no egg boxes in them days, so he put his eggs in a wooden box full of sawdust, you had to feel for them when someone wanted to buy some. When I come home he'd shut the old 'orse out, rack him up, then we would go back up to Albert's 'ouse and have a boiled egg.

He was the area potato manager during the war, he was in charge and all the potatoes had to go through 'im. He was dealing with the allocations for shops and with the farmers an' all. *Archie Shepherd*

Albert Brown's Grocer Shop, Brook Street, son Robert standing in the doorway, c. 1932.

Dear's Cycle shop, Arlesey Road

My husband Stan ran the bicycle shop and people came from miles around, he took over the shop when he was about 19. His grandfather started the business. They used to sell penny-farthing bikes and they used to come here for a 'bamboo' – thruppence an hour to ride about. Part of the bike was made of bamboo and that's what gave it the name, it was a penny-farthing effort. We used to glide along on them, we often went to the station, and Hinxworth, and Ashwell Spring. *Mill Dear neé Smith*

Edgar Saunderson, Hitchin Road

Edgar Saunderson carried on his business in a shop built of corrugated iron which stood in the Folly, at the top of Hitchin Road near the Methodist Chapel. It had two rooms, a haberdashery-cum'-tailor's shop in the front, and a men's hairdressing salon at the back. That's where the undertakers is now.

Edgar's price was tuppence, called a 'tuppenny all off'. His scissors were not very sharp and tended to pull one's hair. It was said that if you could keep from crying, Edgar would keep you from laughing. One day Will Tookey went to Edgar for a haircut and when he was leaving he said, 'Cheerio, Edgar, I shan't be seeing you again'. 'Why not?' asked Edgar. To which Will replied, 'Well you've pulled them all out by the roots haven't you!' *Bert Hyde*

I used to go down to old Edgar's for a shave. He used to keep this pot on top of the old coke stove and would dip the brush in the top, the soap was at the bottom, he never cleaned it. He sold everything there, the corduroys that men used to have, and the thick old vests. The stuff wasn't in boxes in those days it was in thick old paper tied up with string. *Edward Bowskill*

The Munts they lived next to the Coach and Horses, they went up to Edgar's shop every Saturday night for a shave. I remember Edgar's alright, tuppence for 'aircut, and when he went to brush the hair off you'd think he owed you a grudge, the brush was that 'ard, oh dear. He was a good tailor, I had a sports jacket made by him once. I don't know how it came about, I saw this material I liked and asked Edgar to make me a jacket, it was a nice one too, all hand-tailored, I think he only charged me 30 bob, something like that. *Sam Pooley*

Turner's General Store, Queen Street

I was born in Queen Street, where Mr Stoten now lives. My mother and father had a general store there, they moved into it when they first got married. They sold a bit of everything, paraffin, sweets, groceries, saucepans and kettles. That was 1912 when they first went into the shop. The busiest night was Saturday night,

Right: Searle's Post Office, c. 1920.

they used to keep open late. At that time of day people hadn't got cars, so the courting couples used to go for a walk and call in the shop and buy half-a-pound of Cadbury's chocolates, they were sold loose in those days. They would take their chocolates and go and sit on the stile and eat them. That was their Saturday night out, in the summer-time. There was a long procession come in there for the chocolates. Everything was loose, even the sugar and flour, it was all in sacks and we used to have to weigh it up. The shop wasn't very big, there were two counters, one for sweets and groceries and the other for bacon and one thing and another. I was about nine years old when we left there and we went to live up High Street. *George Turner*

Nottage Bakers, Brook Street

Marnie Nottage had a little shop down Brook Street, and that was near Westrope's, the wine shop, near the Primitive Methodist. The baker for Nottage used to have an old Harley Davidson combination, and he would deliver the bread round in that, we called him the 'midnight baker'; he used to come around at 10 to 11 o'clock at night. There was nobody to help him; he had to get up early to knead the dough. He had a great bushy moustache, tiny iron specs and his face was as sharp as a needle. He was so thin – the poor blighter was probably worked to death. *Doug Flitton*

Marnie Nottage used to deliver bread of a Saturday night round Letchworth by horse and cart. They used to call the baker Jack-in-the-box, he had ginger hair. Before they delivered by motorbike he used fly around, cap on, on his bike with a bread basket and when

Nottage Bakers, Brook Street, 1921. Mrs Nottage on the cart.

he emptied the basket, he'd go back for more. He never went home, he just used to sleep in the bakehouse on the flour bins. *Edna Darton née Gentle*

Marnie Nottage ran the bakehouse in Brook Street, her mother used to have a confectionery shop. She never turned us away, we used to give her pennies and ha'pennies and she would keep it all till Christmas. And when we went there she would say, 'Now come on you children, make up your minds'. We used to have our hot-cross buns delivered to us first thing in the morning, hot from the ovens. *Florence Phillips née Gentle*

Cordwell Shepherd, Butcher, The Green

Cordie Shepherd used to be on The Green, where the fishing tackle shop is now. I used to take newspapers there for him to wrap his meat up in and he'd give me a penny a pound for them. He would put clean paper in between. *Jack Brown*

My dad was one of twelve children, they lived in a thatched cottage in the meadow opposite where Smyth's used to be. They used to go down to Bowman's mill, net his fish of a night-time, bring them back to old Cordie Shepherd's, give him the fish and he used to give them meat for it. *Emily Cardell née Milliard*

John and Bessie Hyde, The Green

Bessie Hyde had a sweet shop on The Green, which was competition for Gentle's shop, and Bessie's husband John also had the front room of a house and he sold sweets. His counter was

Above left: Talbots with the Post Office next door, which moved from the High Street to Regent Street in 1945.

Mrs Hyde in front of her Pork Shop, The Green, c. 1943.
Below: W Day and Sons, Green-grocer, Regent Street, c. 1940. Pete Day standing in the doorway.

Top right: F Levitt & Son, Drapers and Grocers, Regent Street. Malcolm Howard, Rosie Mann and Louie Brown standing in front of the shop.

Bottom right: Westrope's wine shop, Brook Street.

littered with spectacles, little old things that pinched on your nose, and little old wire spectacles. You simply went there if you couldn't see, and kept trying on the spectacles until you found a pair that suited. *Doug Flitton*

F Pearmain, Baker and Confectioner, The Green

I was born in the bakehouse, we moved to the Crown when I was 14. My father took over from his dad. He was in the police force first, then went into the army, in the Royal Army Service Corp. as a baker. When he came out of there in 1918 and my parents got married he took the bakehouse on, until 1939. After that it closed and was just a private house.

My mother used to cook the dinner for the fair people in them ovens, and Mrs King that used to keep the shop, she used to make cakes and bring them down to us and bake them in Mum's ovens. Lots of people would bring their cakes in for baking.

My father went to church twice a day. He came home and changed and started making the dough, it was all done by hand. It was 4½d for a loaf. He won a first prize from Hovis for his baking. I remember he used DCL yeast, and I think it was Bowman's flour. *Mary Westrope née Pearmain*

On Sunday we used to go from our home on The Green to the Baptist Chapel. We would take our joint of meat and the Yorkshire pudding in a milk can, and we would call in at France Pearmain's, leave it in there, and then carry on to chapel. The oven was still hot from cooking the bread and they used to push that lot in. When it was time for the pudding, the wife would pour it all round the meat. When we came out from chapel, we would collect it already cooked, so we didn't have to wait for a meal when we got home. They used to charge us thruppence. *Doug Flitton*

Not only was France Pearmain the baker, but he was the coalman too, black and white trade we used to call it. My first wife, Ivy, was Pearmain's niece. *George Shepherd*

Folly Tobacco Stores, Hitchin Road

Folly Tobacco Stores started in about 1938, in the former Co-op shop. Not only did they sell tobacco, but also sweets, cards and books. It was also a lending library, they had 250 books to choose from at 2d per week. Then there was the ice-cream for which James Hallworth was renowned.

During the war, when sugar was hard to get, my father used to go out in the dead of night and get this sugar from somewhere. He stored it under the floorboards, in the bedroom above the shop. This particular bedroom had a lovely Canadian-pine, secret nailed floor, when you took the carpet up there was not a mark to be seen on this floor, no nails. Anyway, Tommy Rutt from Wilbury farm, (Stan Hyde my uncle used to call him the 'Shah of Persia'), told me that the ceiling in the shop was bowed with the weight of the sugar. *John Hallworth*

Jim Hallworth carried on making ice-cream all through the war years, he made a good ice-cream. My brother was well in with Jim Hallworth, we very often had ice-cream at home during the war years. One day we'd got visitors from Luton, so I went down to Jim's for some ice-cream, brought it back and their eyes stood out like bloody organ stops. *Sam Pooley*

Chapter 5

On the Land

Between 1848 and 1849, the Enclosure Act transformed farming from tiny strips of land to larger fields which in turn led to a more efficient way of cultivation. From 1870 onwards there was a sharp decline in the price of corn due to the influx of cheap wheat from America. For instance, in 1867 wheat had been roughly 64s 5d per quarter but in 1893 had dropped to 25s 7d.

This prompted a trend towards market gardening for the smaller farms, Stotfold being no exception. Speedy distribution was aided by the coming of the railway which enabled the produce to be sold through the London markets of Covent Garden, Spittalfields and Borough markets. A variety of crops were grown, all labour-intensive, including onions (Bedfordshire Champion being a well know variety), carrots, cabbages, Brussels sprouts, sugar beet, beans and peas. Increased mechanisation came to the larger farms as they turned from horse-drawn to steam-drawn ploughs, and invested in threshing, binding and mowing machines.

In 1908 Bedfordshire County Council acquired about 450 acres of agricultural land in Stotfold for small holdings, namely the Manor and Bury Farms. Most of it was let out to individual tenants, but the bulk of Manor Farm (135 acres), including the farmyard, was let to the newly formed Stotfold Smallholders Co-operative. The Society was founded on 24 April 1908, its main objective being the creation and promotion of smallholdings within the village. In the beginning there were about 34 members farming 113 acres of land, a further 24 acres being kept for pasture. The bulk of the cultivation was done on a contract basis, the Society having bought horses and employed two men for this purpose, but eventually many of the members aquired their own teams of horses. The Society is still going strong, the difference being that members now own tractors and other pieces of up-to-date equipment. Of course the advantage of such a society was, and still is, that the County Council only had to deal with one tenant instead of the many individuals. If any of the tenant farmers were unable to pay their rent then the Society helped out; the Council was never out of pocket.

In Brook Street there was a chap named Jimmy Saunders, he didn't have much ground of his own, but he had quite a lot of horses. He used to do contract ploughing, this was before my time, in about the late 1800's. He employed quite a lot of men. In the farmyard next to where Joe Millard lives there was stables. The men were supposed to get there at five o'clock in the morning to feed and water the horses and groom them. Well last thing at night Saunders used to put new candles in the stables so they could light up when they came in the morning. But they couldn't find out how he knew when they were late, because he didn't used to be there himself. Eventually they twigged; he put a new candle in every night so that when they lit up in the morning and he came round at seven o'clock, he could tell which of them was late because their candle hadn't burnt down quite so far. Once they found out, if they were late, they always used to cut a bit off the candle!

There used to be an old chap who lived in the Crofts. His name was Pickle, I don't remember his proper name. When they were out of work they used to follow Alex Smith's threshing tackle. That used to take all winter to go round Stotfold and thresh everybody's stacks out. This particular year Pickle was following the machine round, and the farmer would perhaps pick half-a-dozen men to work and the rest would clear off. Wherever they went that year they had been paying them sixpence an hour. This was until they got to Joe Randall's, that was always the last port of call. When he used to pay them, they didn't put the money in packets; they would bring a little table out into the rickyard and put piles of money on it, and you would go along and hold your hand out. 'Course they already worked out how much they had got to come. When Joe paid them they all looked, but some of them daren't say nothing, then Pickle looked at his and realised Joe had only paid them

Members of the Stotfold Small-holders Co-operative, c. 1910.

fivepence an hour. So he went back to the table and said, he stuttered, 'W-w-ell M-m-r R-r-randall, you always have had a good name, b-b-but I'm b-b-buggered if I can s-s-see it'. *George Turner*

My father was an 'urdle maker, he used to go round the farms making these 'urdles. When he hadn't got any wood to make 'urdles he used to 'ang gates for Alex Smith at Grange Farm, rough carpentry it was called. When he hadn't got that to do he would help Donny Kitchener, and cut all round his hedgerows, and the bundles of wood he would take round the village Saturday afternoon and sell them.

Skinny Jack used to go around with the old threshing machines, you would always see him up the top there. His job was cutting the band off the sheaf before feeding it into the drum. *Wally Larkins*

My father was a smallholder in the late 1930s. We had two horses and carts and we reared a few pigs and chickens. We grew wheat, oats, potatoes, peas, marrow, beans and sugar beet. We grew wheat where Vaughan Road is, and besides the wheat there was a mass of red poppies. It seems we have gone full circle as recently along Arlesey Road there's been a field of poppies.

Connor Gentle lifting sugar beet,
Stone Road, 1935.

The pea-picking was in late June and early July, this was done by hand. The women would get up at four o'clock in the morning and arrive at the field with their small stools and lunch. They were paid piece-work for the number of weighed bags. A spring steelyard was used for the weighing as it had a hook to insert in the bag. When I was young I used to like going after the women had finished and finding all the pods left over and then I'd be eating peas for the rest of the day.

The sugar beet was lifted by a special plough pulled by horses and then the beet would be picked up, the leaves chopped off, and put into heaps which were covered with the leaves to keep out the frost. Then, on a given date specified by the sugar refiners, the heaps would be loaded into a cart and transported to Arlesey Station.

The workers in the field often took a Bedfordshire Clanger[1] for their beaver[2], or a bit of cheese and a hunk of bread with an onion, and they'd use their shet-knife[3] to cut it up. They usually had cold tea which was in an enamel container with a round top and a carrying handle. They would keep this in a wicker basket which they would sling over their back while they worked. Or if that was too uncomfortable, they'd put it in a sack and sling the sack over.

1   a pasty, half jam and half meat
2   mid-day break
3   clasp-knife

Anyone going Brusslin' would always tie a sack round themselves to keep the cold wind from their back. Everything was done by hand in those days. A lot of women worked on the land, my mother often went stone picking. *Claude Ingrey*

My grandfather's name was Legate and he was an 'orsekeeper. He used to get up at five o'clock in the morning, seven days a week, no holidays mind you. He used to go out and feed the horses, come home and have his breakfast, then go at seven o'clock and take the horses out ploughing until about two o'clock in the afternoon. He worked for Alex Smith at Grange Farm, but before that he worked for Ern Dear.

In my younger days there were some buildings along Common Road that used to be a chaff house, where they used to thresh the corn. They either had an elevator to stack the straw for animal feed or they had a chaff cutter on the end which used to cut the chaff into short lengths for cattle feed, horses, cows, etc. When we were boys we used to go and tread the chaff. We'd take our shoes and stockings off and keep treading the chaff to push it down ready for the next load. *Jack Brown*

After my father finished working for Pateman's, he had his own ground along what they call the Merle, the cart track opposite Brook Street. He farmed it all himself, he didn't have anybody

A farm wagon with two sets of wheels, used for carrying heavy loads.

John Chambers with some of the chicks he reared.

working for him. He grew Brussels, sugar beet, potatoes and peas. The women used to come and pick the peas for sixpence a bag. His produce used to go to Covent Garden and Spittalfields, Charlie Smith's father did the haulage. Sometimes he used to throw the stuff away because it wasn't worth paying the haulage. They had a couple of landing stages, one was by Ingrey's. It was like a platform on stilts, so that the lorry could drive up to it and the tail board was in line with the platform. It was much easier to load the goods onto the lorry. They also had landing stages for churns of milk, there was one at the top of Vaughan Road at the back.

We used to store our potatoes in a pit with straw on top and quite often we would open it up only to find that the rats had beaten us to the potatoes. They used to do that a lot. You could usually grow enough potatoes to store in a pit and keep the family going all year. We used to keep carrots in sand.

Working on the land was hard work. My dad never had a watch, but he always knew what time it was, he knew exactly what time to go home for his dinner. On dad's ground, he had potatoes one side and Brussels planted the other. When they got to about two or three inches we'd go and pick them in bundles of a score. Then we would plant them over the field, after a good rain, otherwise you had to get a bucket and get the water from the brook and bring it all the way up the field and that was about 150 yards. You would dib it in, then set it down with your foot. When you'd set two or three score you went to the brook for the water and watered them in. You'd have to do that for 5 or 6,000 plants. When the field was ploughed, you had to rake it all down – my father would think nothing of digging an acre by hand. You would mark it out with this rake so that you knew where to put your Brussel plants. If you set them too close you couldn't get in to pull the Brussels off. We would dig sugar beet with a two-pronged fork. *Alan Dear*

Times were hard, and if you wanted anything you had to save up and scrimp and scrape. I went to work on the fields in the summer time, pea-picking. I worked all one week when Bert was a boy and I earnt 27s 3d and I thought, the Lord's been good to let me earn this. That weekend Bert was going on a choir outing so I gave him the money. I thought the Lord's let me earn it so I'll let the boy have a good time. He bought his brother a 2s 11d watch and he kept it for years, and every time he took it out of his pocket I used to think – that was bought with money that I earned. *Doll Gentle née Peacock*

At pea-picking one time, Doll Gamp come over faint and somebody called out for some water, but nobody was prepared to give up their water because it was so hot. They looked in her bag and found some Tizer which they used to revive her! *Edward Bowskill*

Top: Stotfold women picking blackcurrants at Delamere Farm, Great Wymondley, 1942.

Middle: A group of workers taking a rest from pea-picking.

Bottom: Women in the onion fields along Taylors Road, c. early 1940s. Bruce Pateman standing behind the women

I left school at 14 and did dung-spreading for my father, in fact, I was doing that before I left school. My father worked for a Dutch firm and he was in charge of the men in England. There were gangs of them digging potatoes, onions, all things like that. They also had gangs going to Jersey to dig the early 'tatters, Sid Gentle and all that. Then my father arranged for me to do a seven-year apprentice with Alex Smith, that didn't appeal to me. Trevor Shepherd, my mate, suggested we go up the Kryn,[1] my father went bonkers. I was only at Alex Smith's for eight or nine months. I went to the Kryn for about a week and no sooner had I started, I was called up because I was no longer in a reserved occupation.

When I worked for Alex, first of all I did early mornings, five o'clock, milking the cows. When we done that and put them out in the meadow, I'd go with Harry Brown, the shepherd boy. When I finished with him I would sometimes go with George Howard driving plough. Alex Smith had his own blacksmith shop in the back, where they would shoe their own horses. He lost his temper with me one day when I addressed his son as Malcolm and not Master Malcolm. He knocked me back and pushed me into the stables. Of course the rest of them thought that was funny.

When I came out of the Army they were offering soldiers an acre of ground and a pig, something like that. I ended up with a piece of land, three acres, in the Merle. I used to send the stuff to Covent Garden. Sugar beet I would send by rail. The potatoes and sprouts I used to sell by the ton, the lorry would come at night and load up. I worked on the land for 14 or 15 years, I had all what is now Roker Park, and six acres over the Merle, I had quite a bit. I had two tractors and I did all my own work. My brother had some land over the Merle and he used to help me and I helped him, he must have had 30 or 40 acres. I employed the women to pick up the potatoes and Brussels. I grew about 15 acres of corn; Peacock did the threshing for me, he worked for Alex Smith. I had seven breeding sows; when they got too old I used to let Bruce Pateman[2] have them. *John Chambers*

When George and Wally Munt's mother died they were looked after by Alice Endersby who was paid by the Poor Law. Their mother used to do all their dumplings on a Saturday night and put them all in the old copper, which was an old cast iron thing in some brickwork. She would light a fire underneath and do enough dumplings for the week. Wally would take them up to the farm and you'd see him sit there at lunch time cutting bits off. *Reg Saunders*

Old Wally Munt, the father, used to work up Buntingford way, he'd walk there. She used to make him seven dumplings so he'd know

1   Kryn and Laby, the iron foundry in Letchworth
2   The slaughterman, see page 103

what day to come home. One week she only put six in so he came home a day early. *Alf Cardell*

Before telephones, Frank Hyde's father, Harry, wrote two letters one week. One was for the vet because the pig wasn't well, and one to the parson to come and preach, and he put them in the wrong envelopes. He told me that himself so I know that was true. *Doll Gentle née Peacock*

Stotfold Soot-Sower

Tom Dear was a soot-sower who broadcast by hand. In those days many tons of London soot came into the district. It was carted in big bags from the local railway station by horse and cart. The bags were dumped in the fields in long rows, 20 to 30 yards apart. Tom had to wait for a nice calm day to begin work. He had a half-moon shaped scuttle strapped round his waist which he filled from each sack, then strode out, arms and legs in perfect unison, in, I might add, a cloud of dust. He often worked, I was told, on moonlit nights and usually started work when the other farm workers were leaving off, if the weather was right. He also had to stop sometimes if the weather turned wrong, and the farmer complained that his neighbour was getting the benefit of his soot! I remember how his very white teeth showed up in his black face when he smiled. My grandmother told me she cleaned her teeth with soot when she was a child!

Tom's long-suffering wife always had the copper on when he got home and he would briefly appear in his long pants as he flung out his soot-stiffened clothes. He would burn these in his garden bonfire when they became too stiff which was no doubt the reason he grew the biggest cabbages and Brussels sprouts I ever saw. His bath water, which he had to empty with a bucket, was put on his wife's flower garden which grew tremendous pansies and carnations. *A W Ingrey. (Reprinted with permission from* This England.)

Cutting corn along Arlesey Road. Claude Ingrey on the tractor, 1948.

Chapter 6

The Day's Work

From 1850 to about 1914 there had always been some industry in the village, if only brick making and milling; the village was never exclusively agricultural.

Coprolite digging and plywood manufacture were both significant industries, but these were not mentioned during the recordings. In the twenty years from 1860 to 1880 up to 29 villagers were employed either digging or sorting coprolite – the petrified droppings of prehistoric animals. It would then be crushed for use as a fertilizer.

The plywood manufacturer Borst Brothers came to Stotfold during the 1939/45 war opening a factory in Taylors Road. Their plywood was used, amongst other things, for Mosquito fighter-bomber aircraft.

Straw Cutting and Plaiting

In Stotfold, straw cutting and plaiting was an important cottage industry, second only, in numbers employed, to agriculture. Production of the straw plait reached its peak in the 1870s, then cheaper imports from China, and later Japan, forced the industry into decline.

The men were mostly responsible for growing and cutting the straw and would sell it on to dealers who purchased the unthrashed stacks of wheat. The best and largest stems were selected and stripped to remove the knots and leaf, sorted and tied into bundles. After cutting, the straw went through a bleaching process.

Plaiting was an ideal occupation for women and young children because it could be done at home. The children were sent to plait school almost as soon as they could walk, generally working in very poor conditions. In the 1851 Census for Stotfold, Jane Gentle, Mary Gentle and Elizabeth Cooper were all listed as 'mistress of a school for straw plait only.' In the mid-1800s, a wife and two children could supplement the husband's agricultural wage of 10 shillings a week by an additional 12 shillings or more.

In those days, years back, there was a lot of poor people in Stotfold, there was nothing for them to do except for a bit of smallholding and straw plaiting. The old girls used to go to Hitchin

Above: Cut straws for plaiting, c. 1906. Alex Smith's barn, Grange Farm, Mr Rowland, centre.

Below: Cut straws, plait and hats on display at Hospital Day. Mr Legate, horseman, Bert Gentle, Mrs Cox and Miss Rhoda Brown on the wagon.

on the wagons on Tuesdays, market day, and they used to bring this straw plait in and sell it on the market to the boys from Luton. *Cecil Edwards*

In the cottages next door to Ivy Lodge, they did straw plaiting, and it all went to Luton for the hat industry. Corn dollies were also made, and they sold well. *Odette Kitchiner née Randall*

My grandmother, who lived on The Green, had what they called a plaiting school. It was a shed and she had to pay tax on the shed because she had got these young girls plaiting in there. And then it would be collected up and go by horse and cart to Hitchin market where it would be bought by the traders. *Winifred Searle*

Mother used to cycle to Luton; relations of ours had a hat factory there. She would come home and bring a big box of hats on the back of her bike for the people around here. *Dorothy Pond neé Nisbet*

I was born at Brook End on the corner of Brook Street. My mother used to cut these straws, she was brought up with it since her mother before her did it. There was like a block of three houses down there, we had two and the middle house was for cutting these straws. She worked with her brother Ted Dear, my uncle. There were three others, Mrs Cox, Mrs Howard and Rhoda Brown, and he used to take straw round on his trolley to a Mrs Hewitt and Mrs Gentle who lived along Dark Lane.

The farmer used to grow the corn. It was stored in Alex Smith's barns and these men used to do what we called 'drawing the straws' and putting it into bundles. Ted used to go and fetch them on his trolley and they stacked them in what we called the big barn, which was the building on the corner. Then the women cut them. The straws would then go out in the other barn and Ted would cut all the tops off, then the straws would come back in again to be what we used to call machined. They used to put them on a sort of sieve thing and sort them all out into their sizes. After the sorting Ted used to do them up into bunches then put them in the steam house to bleach them, then they would come back to be sorted again. Then he would bunch them all up with string and put them in great big bags and then take them to Arlesey station to go to Luton. Then he would fetch back the coal from Arlesey station. I used to help my mum do the straws. I often got told off by Ted because I hadn't cut them straight. I think the women used to get paid according to how many bundles they used to cut in a week. *Edna Darton neé Gentle*

My husband, Percy's, aunt, used to cut straws all the week long. Her house would be full of straws all the week, then Friday she would clear it all up. She had a big barn outside where she would steam them, and then she used to split them and they would take them to Hitchin to sell them. *Doll Gentle neé Peacock*

My grandmother, down the Common, she cut straws and a chap called Moke, she used to let him sleep up in her loft, he would wet all these straws when she had got them in bundles. They used to have this huge great wooden thing with sulphur or something and they had to dip these straws when they had got them cut, and then they used to take them to Hitchin market every Tuesday. One day she asked me to fetch Moke's pot for his tea, and that was a two-pound jam jar. Finch Gentle, he had that double-fronted house down on the Common, he used to go every week to Hitchin and take these straws. *Maud Castle neé Seymour*

Milling

Taylor's Mill

Of the three mills, Taylor's, Randall's and Astwick, only Taylor's was not mentioned in the recorded conversations as it stopped operating in the early 1900s and is now a private residence. Erected on the site of a previous mill in the mid-18th century, it incorporates two cottages under its long roof. Pryors, the brewers, of Baldock purchased the mill in 1795 from the Lyttons of Knebworth who were lords of Stotfold manor, and sold it on to J G Fordham of Odsey, near Ashwell. In the Stotfold riots of 1830 the rioters threatened to burn it down. It was then described as an extensive corn and seed mill. The mill foreman for Mr Fordham was John Taylor and by 1861 his son John Taylor jnr., was milling there on his own account. He left the mill around 1880. The last miller there was a Mr William Bancroft.

Astwick Mill

On 12 March 1857, Samuel Bowman of Rook Tree Farm purchased Astwick Mill from George Waldock. The conveyance of the property described Astwick as 'the newly built brick and slated water corn mill with stage bins, machinery, gears and tackle and nine pairs of French stones, worked by a fall of 20 feet'. Samuel Bowman's son James took on the running of the mill at the age of 24.

The mill was converted from stone grinding to roller milling in 1891 when six small roller mills were purchased to replace the French stones. This, combined with supplementing waterpower by steam power, enabled James Bowman to become a pioneer of roller milling among country millers. He was described by his grand-daughter Ina as being 'over six foot and very strong, he would show off by carrying

Taylor's Mill.

two 2½ hundredweight sacks, one under each arm across the mill'.

Ernest and Harry, James's sons became involved in the family business and in 1901 opened the Station Mill at Hitchin. Edward Smyth, who had married James Bowman's youngest daughter, took over the running of the mill at Astwick which continued in production until 1922.

My father used to have to get down to the mill by six o'clock, he cycled there and back for breakfast, which we had at twenty-to-eight every morning, then he cycled back again. He'd cycle back again for lunch which was an hour, and then he would get home at six to half-past. When father first went to work at the mill he earnt £178 a year.

The men were wonderful with me at the mill. They let me do anything I liked, but they made me do it properly. They produced flour and animal feed, bran and crushed oats for horses. It was all horses in those days, they used to keep about eight horses down there and the steam wagon. Nanny's father, Will Dilley, he used to drive the wagon, but I was never allowed to go with him because he drank, the horses used to bring him home; I used to go delivering flour with the Pooleys. *Ina Roberts née Smyth*

My old man finished up as what they called roller man, setting the rollers and everything, they'd got to be set just right. He told me this tale about the manager who swore blind that the rollers weren't set just right, there was a bigger gap one side than the other, so the flour was coarser from one side than the other. The guv'nor called my old man up to the office and said, 'I want you to

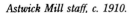
Astwick Mill staff, c. 1910.

Astwick Mill with the boathouse in the foreground.

go down to that roller and take out a handful of flour from the right-hand side then take a handful from the left-hand side, and bring them up to me'. Well the old man took two handfuls out of one side and took them up to the office and laid it out. The guv'nor said, 'I knew very well you ain't got them rollers set right'. My old man enjoyed that. *Sam Pooley*

After handing over the running of Astwick Mill to his two sons and son-in-law, James Bowman devoted his time to other things. His second daughter, Gertrude, married an eminent authority on musical stringed instruments. Characteristically, James installed in his mill a mechanism for continually passing a bow over each string of new violins, to improve their resonance as if by years of playing. He also experimented on violin varnishes.

When we were very young we would walk down to Astwick, which was quite a walk. Sarah, Nanny's mother, who lived in the cottages at the bottom of the lane, used to give us brown sugar on a new crust of bread, she made her own bread. That was a great treat, we loved going to see Sarah. There was a beautiful walled garden down at the mill. Grandfather used to grow palma violets, he had a greenhouse and he grew beautiful grapes. And at the bottom he used to have what he called his den and in there he experimented with varnishes for violins. I didn't like going in there so I spent my time with granny. *Joan Smyth*

In his den grandfather had an enormous tub of fishmeal he used to feed his violets on. He couldn't reach right to the bottom so I had to do it. He would give me a little enamel bowl with a handle and he then held me upside-down by my legs, and I had to collect the fishmeal in the bowl. One day he dropped me in. Mother said that I smelt for six months after that. *Ina Roberts neé Smyth*

Randall's Mill

I left school, at 13 I think it was, and I went to work down Randall's mill, 10 shillings a week. I had to clean the shoes for Ruth and George and I had to take them to school in a pony and cart. George went to school at Radwell, Reverend Waller was his schoolmaster, and Ruth went to Grove House School in Baldock. But I never fetched her home, her father had got an old T-Ford car and he used to bring her home. During the day I used to harness the donkey, they had a donkey as well, and go and fetch a load of mangel-wurzels. They used to have a contraption that you put the wurzels in one at a time, turn a handle and that ground them up, and they mixed them up with the chaff, that was feed for the horses. Another thing I used to do, they'd got a big machine in there, and what he done was 'dress' corn. An old man named Freddy Gentle worked there. I used to have to turn the handle and he put the corn in. It used to blow all the dirt out of the corn. I had to collect the eggs up and Eb Randall, the miller, would come to me some mornings and say, 'Shepherd, there's a dozen ducks' eggs up the river, go and fetch them'. I used to have to wash these ducks' eggs ready for them to take to Hitchin market, and hens' eggs.

When I worked at the mill there was Frank Bishop, he was the foreman, and Frank Cooper was the labourer, and there was two men in the mill and two men on the horses and cart, Fred Gentle and me, that's all the men that worked there.

I used to like Eb Randall. I'd go shooting with him, doing the beating. We would go in his old Ford car. *George Shepherd*

I understand that J Arthur Rank which is Hovis Rank now, had their first flour ground at Randall's mill. That was when they had the new steam mill built, it was built on the strength of the business they received from J Arthur Rank, but they then decided to do it themselves. After that the mill never did work to capacity. That engine went for scrap. Eb Randall went broke in 1928 and Northern's stood in for him. *David Shepherd*

Above: Randall's Mill.

Below: George Randall with the rear of the mill in the background.

Brickmaking in Stotfold

In 1850 there were two brick-kiln sites in production in Stotfold: one at Wrayfields to the east of the road which used to run to Caldecote, and another at Astwick Road bridge. Going to Astwick from Stotfold, it is the last field on the left-hand side, south of the river. It is still known locally as the 'brickyard'. There was also an associated brick-kiln on the other side of the road.

Astwick Road Brick-kilns

George Waldock, the Astwick miller, owned the brick-kilns at Astwick Road bridge which operated for just seven or eight years from 1847 to 1855. There is no trace of a clay pit in the vicinity so the question arises, where did he get his clay from? In 1847 he built the new Astwick mill, and, at about the same time, cut a different channel for the river with the object of securing depth for his new overshot waterwheel and a free run of water downstream. There is a 20 foot drop at the waterwheel, the altered channel has a steep embankment in places and is half a mile long. Cutting this channel must have necessitated shifting many tons of earth and, as the New Cut runs right by the two Astwick Road brick-kiln sites, it does not seem improbable that when digging it he came upon clay suitable for brickmaking and used it for that purpose. Birdy Cooper, whose grandmother used to keep the old Peewit public house in Astwick Road (now no. 81) before 1900, said that the Peewit was built from the bottom of the river, and he may well have been right. George Waldock died in December 1854 and the brick-kilns were sold in 1857, by which time both kilns had ceased production.

Wrayfield Brick-kiln

Wrayfield brick-kiln had already been working for at least 19 years when it was acquired by James Lambert in 1850. He was followed by his son Alfred who continued to run it until about 1900. They both lived in Brick-kiln Cottage (1849), now Wrayfield House, where the date and former name can still be seen on the front of the house. Their stock brick was hand-made, grey and of excellent quality and was known as the 'Stotfold Brick' in the local building trade. When recovered from demolitions, it commands a good premium even today. It was used in the construction of many Stotfold buildings, including the former Old Baptist Chapel in Rook Tree Lane (1857), the Methodist Church in High Street (1867) and 24 Regent Street (1884).

Redhouse and Company, the old established firm of Stotfold builders, bought the Wrayfield brick-kiln in about 1900 and two years later built numbers 1 and 3 Wrayfield in the field close by the brick-kiln. One of these houses may well have been for the brick-burner who had to be readily available to control the firing of the bricks, a process which took several days to complete. The Wrayfield brick-kiln closed down some time after the start of the First World War so ending over 80 years of brickmaking in Stotfold.

I knew an old chap who used to work in the brick yard at Wrayfield and he was telling me about it. They used to burn red bricks and white bricks. The white bricks he said you could put them in the kiln and light the fire and leave them and they'd burn all right. But when they were burning red bricks he had to stop there all night because he had to keep feeding the fire a bit at a time; you

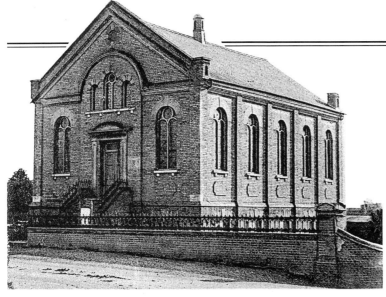

The Wesleyan Chapel, High Street, built 1867 with bricks from the Wrayfield Brick-kiln, known in the trade as the 'Stotfold Brick'.

couldn't overdo it, otherwise they were no good. The red bricks were far more difficult. There was another chap and when he was a lad all he did was walk back and forwards to the Coach and Horses with a couple of gallon jars to fetch the beer for the others. And he said he used to walk down there in his bare feet. *George Turner*

Brewing

Flitton Brothers, Stotfold Brewery

My grandfather started brewing and baking where Pearmain's used to be. Grandfather had three sons; there was George, Frank and Cyrus, my father. My father never went into the brewery, George and Frank carried on with it. I think it was somewhere in 1949 that the business closed.

I was very interested in the brewery, although I never did anything in it. As a boy I was always determined to get round there when it started up each morning at about five o'clock. A chap named Bill Brown, he married a Bandy, he was like a gaffer in the bottling and brewing side, and Bram Castle, he did the heating side, the stoking of the boilers. They would start the place up at five o'clock. One night I slept with all my clothes on so that I could be round there in time, I cut up Ginn's Lane (Oliver's Lane) and cut along the hedge inside and got to the brewery that way, I didn't want to go past the house in case I was seen.

There was a gas generator which they put coke into, then there was this thing you used to wind the handle for bellows and blow this coke to get it going to force the gas up. Then it was piped to a gas engine with two big fly wheels, with a belt on to drive all the machinery. Once they got the gas up they used to get hold of these fly wheels and turn them around, and eventually all the machinery sprung into life. The steam side was for heating the water.

Below: Flitton's first brew house, in the barns to the right of the picture. This later became Pearmain's Bakery.

Right: Flitton's Brewery staff, c. 1937.

Far right: Flitton's Brewery Dray and float, Edwin Auburn with the reins.

A man named Ted Charles was the barrel man, he used to purify all these barrels out with steam before the beer was added. I don't think the barrels were made locally, there was probably a 'hooper' there who repaired them if the bands went or the wood got a bit rough.

Nellie Circuit used to be a bottle washer. There used to be a huge wheel that went into a tank which was full of water and a steam pipe going in there to heat the water, and the wheel that was inside was made to take the bottles. She used to put the bottles on and the wheel would move round with the weight and bottles would get washed out in the tank. Then, when it came up the other side, she would take the bottles out and she had a spindle with a brush on and she would put the bottles on there and clean the inside of the bottle.

My cousin, Frank's son, he went into the brewery one day and there used to be a pipe there running over a doorway that had ammonia in it which acts as a freezing agent. Like a chump he climbed up on something and put his tongue on this pipe; he no sooner did that than his tongue froze to the pipe. Fortunately he didn't try to jump down or it would have ripped his tongue out. This Bill Brown saw it and told him to stay where he was, he got hot water and gradually thawed it off, so that he could free his tongue.

My father used to go round there, and this Bram Castle, he used to have to go upstairs to the top and feed the malt (it was a type of corn) down this chute and they used to grind it all up. I was up there with him where he was chuting it down and I could see him keep picking up some in his hand and putting it in his mouth. Being a kid I didn't see that he got the goodness out of the corn and spat the rest out. I swallowed it all, I went home and I was doubled up with pain. My parents couldn't make out what it was. It swells up inside you.

The strongest beer was 'Stingo'. Uncle Frank brewed some special stout that they used to do, and they entered it into the Brewers' Exhibition in London, and this stout got second prize, which was a great 'leg up' for the firm. With that my uncle put on a supper for all the employees to celebrate the occasion. I went to that, of course they had the stout at the supper. *Doug Flitton*

Bill Brown worked down Flitton's, he was cellar foreman. He'd put a case of Stingo's on one side and leave 'em there for twelve months. I went down there once with Bill File, we was only about 17. He fetched this crate of Stingo out and we had two or three of them and we come home with two left legs.

At one time Flitton's used to supply beer to pubs in London. When I was working nights, I used to finish six o'clock on a Saturday morning like, go home for a bit of breakfast, then go up London with my mate Bill File who used to drive the lorry. There were several pubs, one I distinctly remember was the White Monkey down Waldorf Street. *Sam Pooley*

Woodyards

R Shepherd & Sons Woodyard

My great-grandfather started the business in 1804 and it was on the go for 160 years. The business passed to my grandfather and then to Don Shepherd, my uncle, who came back from the war in 1917 when my grandfather died, to carry on the business. From then on it ran as R Shepherd & Sons, by Jim, my dad and Don. The 'R' stood for Ruth my grandmother. At that time, 1917, our customers included people like Bruce Pateman, Smyth, down where Brayes Manor is now, Struthers, down Astwick, Baxter & Worboy's, local builders, Desoutt from Mill House, Radwell, Cedric Castle from the New Inn, Aubrey Castle and Northern.

Dad and Uncle Don built it up into a thriving timber business, before that they were more interested in the wheelwright side of it. In the yard out there, there is a big saw pit where they used to cut the timber. I don't ever remember it working. They got their supplies of wood mostly from the farmers, round about. In the early days collecting the timber was done by horses. They used to keep all the horses down the timber yard which is now G & L's builder's yard. They went to Letchworth, Baldock, anywhere in the

Top: Shepherd's wheelwright shop, c. 1930.

Bottom: Shepherd's Woodyard c. 1940.

surrounding district. My dad used to get up at four o'clock in the morning to get the horses ready to be on the road by six to go down to Old Warden. That's where they got most of their decent timber as against the hedgerow stuff you would buy from the farmer.

The horses pulled a timber gig which was a two-wheeled machine with a long pole on it and a hump; instead of the axle being straight, it had a big hump. They used to push over the tree, put a chain around the middle of the tree, pull the handle down and this hump used to come up and just lift the tree off the ground so that they could move it. They never used to load it as such on to a trailer. It was just lifted up off the ground, then horses used to pull it.

Different timbers were used for making the wheel. Elm for the hub, oak for the spokes and ash or elm for the fellies, but they preferred ash. They used to make carts. They did work for lots of farmers in the area.

I can go back to when George Saunders, that would be Reg Saunder's grandad, worked for Shepherd's. In the wages book for 1933, W G Saunders which was old George, wheelwright, he got £1 16s a week. Albert Scott, he was classed as a carter, he went out and carted timber in, got £1 15s, and a wheelwright's labourer earnt 15s a week. They used to reckon it took a week to make a wheelbarrow, before machinery came about, and they used to charge 25s.

George Saunders worked for my dad and uncle for 66½ years. He retired on 3 December 1945. He often used to come up odd times after that to do odd jobs. He used to have a big sit-up-and-beg bike, and at the back where the spindle went through the hub there was a step. You stepped on it from the back and scooted it along, I can remember him doing that.

When they got electricity they went more over to converting timber into anything that was required, such as elm coffin boards, gateposts, gates, I suppose the cart side stopped in about 1940 before the war. They built up the other side of getting timber in, buying 200 to 300 trees, they would render whatever came along, it would be converted into anything anyone wanted. Good elm would be sold to Ercol for furniture, good oak would go for church work to a bloke in Birmingham, ash was supplied to another chap in Birmingham, for the Morris Traveller bodies. Then there was the BBC at Bedford. The Bedford Bat Company had supplies of short pieces of ash for making hockey sticks, rounder bats, baseball bats. Willow would go down to St Neots where they made the cricket bats.

We used to cut hundreds and hundreds of railway sleepers. The railway would send somebody down and they would turn every one over to make sure there was no bark on it and he would put his stamp on the end of it, then we would put them on a lorry and cart them down to what is Arlesey brick yard. There used to be a little crane in a siding and we used to load them on there. *David Shepherd*

Larkin's Woodyard

An old man named Jimmy 'ayley started us up in business years ago. This bit of ground was going opposite the Stag with four old cottages on it. He went and bought it for £300. We pulled all the old cottages down. Verdy Sale and Albert Scott used to help me weekends and nights to build me a long big shed 84-foot long and 28-foot wide, all ready for working. I'd got £9 to start the business. Dick Sole and George Smith, they came to work for me for a pound a week. My missus helped in the woodyard; she used to saw the wood up if anybody wanted a bag of wood and she helped make the 'urdles. We came out of the woodyard in the early 50s. *Wally Larkins*

Coleman Foundry Equipment

Turby Gentle built the Coleman's factory. Then Coleman took it over, he originally ran a factory at Letchworth, which he transferred from there to Stotfold. Then Anderson bought it off Coleman, they made all types of foundry equipment, moulding machines, etc.

During the war they were getting what prices they liked for anything they did, they were in clover then. Of course after the

Larkin's saw mill located in the barn foreground right, where hurdles and chestnut fencing were made. A second barn was located opposite the Stag public house, further down Brook Street.

Lunch break at Coleman's Foundry. Mrs Patrick, the fortune-teller serving behind the counter.

war, it had to be put on a peace time basis. After the war I was approached by Mr Anderson who asked me to run it. So in 1945 I took on the job of Superintendent and stayed with the company for 16½ years. We used to employ about 60 people. If you can imagine when the war finished everywhere stopped, there was no work for anybody anywhere. You couldn't get skilled labour to do the jobs, I had to train quite a few of them up.

During my time there it was taken over by another company, and in 1959 it closed for good and all the machinery was moved to this company's other factory in Oldham. *Bert Jeffs*

Builders

Samuel Redhouse

Samuel Redhouse was born at Fulborn, Cambridgeshire, in 1833 and set up his building enterprise in Stotfold some time before 1869. For many years the firm was based in Baldock Road at Salisbury House, so-called because the firm carried out considerable building work at Hatfield House, the home of Lord Salisbury. Samuel's son John, who at one time lived at 'Rhee side', took over the business from his father, but John's son Stan did not take to the building trade: he farmed at Black Horse Farm near the old Compasses public house at Baldock. Redhouse and Company did a fair amount of building in Stotfold, including the cemetery chapel. They also built The Avenue in 1921, which was part of Lloyd George's, 'houses fit for heroes to live in', after the 1914–18 war. The Avenue houses were the first council houses in Stotfold and that was certainly a landmark.

The first original Redhouse came to Stotfold to build at the Three Counties Hospital. That was Sam and Jack's father, Sam. The son Sam was the architect. Jack was the builder. When the old man first came to Stotfold he lodged at what is now 1 Norton Road. He was a bit more affluent than some and had a donkey to ride to work on. At that time of day when they were building the Three Counties they set a medda' on one side for those that went to work by horse, so they could graze. *George Turner*

My grandfather used to do a lot of work for Lord Salisbury and the people at Knebworth, Lytton. When he came to Stotfold he took over the brickyard, (Wrayfield), he was a very wealthy man. They had a big office right in the yard by the house. He'd sit in his dining room all the men who worked for him had to come into the yard and sign themselves in and out. He'd sit there and say, 'Come on, come on, it's six o'clock you ought to be out there working'. He used to make sure all the men were in before he sat down for his breakfast. *Evelyn Blaker née Edwards, Samuel Redhouse's grand-daughter.*

Grandfather built that big mill at Hitchin for the Bowman's. All those bricks from the brickyard in Stotfold were carted by horse and cart to Baldock Station, put on a train to Hitchin and then they were picked up from there, the mill was built just outside the station yard. When he built the town hall, Hitchin, the same thing happened. He also built the police station down Bancroft and Spur's in the market-place which is all gone now, that was a big store. *Cecil Edwards, Samuel Redhouse's grandson*

I used to work for Stan Redhouse at Baldock on the farm for years. The old man Redhouse he came to Stotfold to work on the asylum, he built a lot in Wimpole House. All the craftsmen worked for him. Will Tookey, Cecil's father, he was a carpenter, he worked in Hatfield House, and they reckoned he worked there for seven years. They say there's some of the finest oak panelling in the country there. My stepfather also worked there, he laid all the stairs in Hatfield House. Redhouse built the Avenue; he had £60,000 to build 62 houses, after The First World War. *Albert Scott*

When Redhouse got on in a big way they got the contract to do the maintenance at Hatfield House. I was talking to a chap who lived down Norton Road who used to work for him, his name was

Houses fit for heroes to live in – the first council houses built in Stotfold by Samuel Redhouse, 1921.

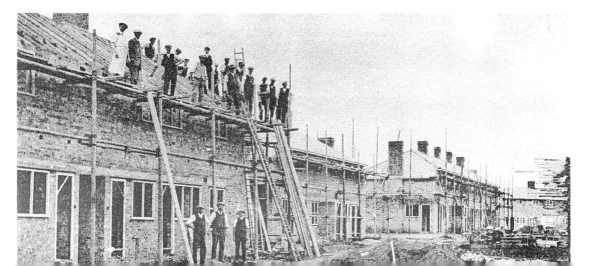

'Trimmer' Brown. He worked for the building side of the business and his job was to drive a horse and cart from Stotfold to Hatfield and back, he used to have to take a load of mortar for the bricklayers because they used to make it on the site. It was lime and mortar in those days, and it had to stand for so long. That was his day's work. When he retired he carried on working for Redhouse doing his garden. *George Turner*

Grandfather Redhouse had a man who used to drive him, Joe Brown, and he wore a coster suit, somebody had given him this suit, it was covered with buttons and I was fascinated with this. that was his best suit, he always wore it to bring the guv'nor out on Sunday. 'Trimmer' Brown was his name. *Evelyn Blaker née Edwards*

Redhouse built this house (180 Hitchin Road) and the one next door. When they were built they cost £436, that was in 1913. My grandfather had the house then, he had a housewarming party in August 1913, and had all his friends in for a booze-up. *Edna Darton née Gentle*

Herbert Gentle

Herbert Gentle was a Stotfold builder of the 30s. Everybody knew him as Turby. He was a member of an old Stotfold family. In his early days he carted hay with a horse and cart. He was a forerunner of the modern developer.

Some of the houses he built stand opposite Pip's Wines and Spirits in High Street, and a comment on them appeared in the Stotfold Review of 1933. 'A new pair of houses has just been built opposite Mr Eli Millard's (High Street). If they continue to build in Mr Bigg's field soon it may be you will no longer be able to enjoy a fine unbroken view of Stotfold Church from Cook's store, (Pip's). Still we have to make room for what some will call improvements.'

He built the Gardens and part of Coppice Mead. Another of his undertakings was Meadow Way, built on the lovely Ray's meadow which was part of the grounds of Stotfold House where our village cricket team played. Everybody was sorry to lose the cricket field. One wit on the Parish Council suggested that the road ought not to be called Meadow Way but Gentle's Folly. It's true that Turby later had his own cricket team that played on the Brittans (the present football pitch), but, when all is said and done, Turby's building on Ray's meadow was the beginning of the end as far as old Stotfold was concerned. In later life he went to live at Clare in Suffolk.

Turby was a man before his time. He used to have Coleman's before they took it over, he made his own covers for drains. When he was building at Baldock, he'd mix cement at Stotfold and take it over in a lorry and tip it out on site. That's what Ready-mix do today. *Bert Hyde*

I worked for Baxter's at Stotfold and Turby Gentle. He came round one night wanting me to play for his football team. He used to play himself, he was getting on then. It was called Gentle's Eleven, they used to play up in Ray's meadow. But of course that meant working for him as well, he wouldn't have nobody unless they worked for him. I agreed and went and worked for him and I played two seasons with him. One of the sayings about Turby was, 'Up she goes like a rocket, another £50 in Turby's pocket.' He was a good man, he did a bit of lay preaching. He did give me the sack because we didn't win many games that season, me and half-a-dozen others.
Biffy Charles

Turby Gentle was my uncle. He got called up in the First World War and that frightened him to death, that's when he took to

Below: Building of the council houses in Regent Street 1925.

Bottom: Norton Road, 'New Town', Stotfold, houses built by Turby Gentle.

religion. He was as bad as everybody else before then. They used to sit in the fields gambling with cards and one of his brothers, Geoff, used to be the look-out in case the coppers came.

Turby bought the bake-house from Doughy Randall and he lived there for quite a time. He carried on baking the bread for a while, then he built that house down Regent Street. *Norman Darton*

Bigg Brothers

Bigg Brothers built the houses in St Mary's Avenue and the old Regent cinema in Arlesey Road. Perhaps one of the largest projects was the Wilbury Hotel. Obtaining permission for its liquor licence was quite a battle which was widely reported at the time, 1938. John Bigg's other claim to fame was that his horse Oxo won the Grand National in 1958.

I bought an old gravel pit near Wilbury Hill for £600. It was in Stotfold, in Bedfordshire, and close to Letchworth which was a 'dry' town, nobody was allowed to sell alcohol. I applied for a licence at Biggleswade Magistrates and I got turned down twice. I did get it eventually, and I built the Wilbury Hotel, my brother Albie was a great man at drawing plans and that sort of thing, Bigg Brothers the company was called. *John Bigg*

George Turner, Builder

My grandfather came from Clifton, and when he started his little building business he used to get quite a lot of work out that way. At that time he employed up to a dozen men, and they always had to walk to work, Arlesey, Clifton or Henlow. So they knew if one another had already left in the morning, when they got to the Wesleyan chapel they would put a stone on the wall. So if anybody came along and sees four stones on the wall, they knew four of them had already gone. And if they got there and there weren't any stones on the wall they would wait for a mate. *George Turner*

Chapter 7

Tradesmen and Craftsmen

Stotfold supported a large number of independent traders who added interest to everyday life as well as providing a much-needed service.

Eustace Ginn, Blacksmith

Many of us children used to watch Mr Ginn the blacksmith shoeing the horses, he also constructed the shoes with his furnace. We used to assist at times, I especially did, in pumping the bellows to keep the furnace going, so that he could heat up the metal and form the horseshoes. Then he would quench them in a tank of water at the side of the furnace. On one occasion, Mr Ginn removed one shoe that he had just quenched in the water and threw it on to the floor. I thought he had dropped it so I went and picked it up, which resulted in a rather badly burned hand. I didn't do the same trick again. *Claude Howard.*

Peter Smith, Blacksmith

Peter Smith was one of the blacksmiths in Stotfold, he had his smithy where Bews electrical shop is today. I used to have to take the horse along for shoeing there and I had to help blow up the fire and hold the horse's head so that he didn't kick Mr Smith. Then I had to ride on the horse to bring him home.

The blacksmiths also used to repair your cartwheels: with wear the tyres used to come loose, these were just iron bands around a wooden wheel. In fact, in the summertime you used to have to take the cart through the pond to get the wood a bit wet to keep the tension on the tyres. If it got too bad you used to take it along to the blacksmith who would then cut a piece out of this iron hoop and then heat-weld it together again. *Claude Ingrey*

A lot of the blacksmith's work was done at night because the farmers needed their horses during the daytime, so they would send them in the evening. The main people were from Norton, Charlie Webb and Ben Parker they both did a lot of contracting and that was all done by horse and cart. The schoolboys used to bring the horses down to Stotfold after tea. They used to ride these big

Top: The Smithy, Rook Tree Lane, run by Eustace Ginn.

Above: Mehew's Blacksmith shop (situated in High Street, at the Queen Street junction), c. 1895.

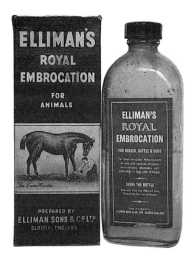

old shire-horses down and back from Norton. 'Course when they went back it was nearly always dark, so they would carry a candle in a jam jar to light the way home. You could soon get lost in the dark. *George Turner*

Owen Hyde, Saddler and Harness-maker

My father was in the army during the First World War and when he came out he took up an apprenticeship with Frank Hayes, the harness maker in Regent Street. It was where Ivan Howard's shop is now. Hayes also had a shop in Chatteris. My father often had to cycle from Stotfold to Chatteris which must be about forty miles.

In 1933 he started up as a harness-maker on his own and kept the shop on the go till about 1960. He repaired harnesses, tarpaulins and binder canvasses. Binders with sails were used to cut the corn. The sails went round and the corn was carried up on what they called canvasses, which was a moving platform. They had laths on, which were wooden strips which went across the canvas. There were two canvasses, they ran over each other and the corn went between them and it was carried up to the binding place on the side of the binder. The corn was packed into sheaths and the arms came over and tied the string round the sheaths, which were then left in the fields, then someone walked round afterwards and what they did was shocking* them. He mended the actual canvas, there were all different sizes for different binders, platforms and elevators. He also repaired the drive-belts from the threshing machines. And he was always repairing the punch-ball they used at the Feast, Mr Cushy used to come with the ball, and get my dad to stitch it up.

He made harnesses, saddles, collars, bridles, school satchels. He made lots and lots of instrument cases for Foster Instruments, with leather and green baize inside, they were for heat registering instruments. All these were to a certain size and they had wooden fittings inside.

He used to sell Elliman's Horse Embrocation, 'orse oils as they called them. Stinks like merry hell, but by gum it don't 'alf get rid of the aches and pains. It's wonderful stuff. It was thick, white and greasy. It was meant to be for horses, but people also used it. Lots of people used to come in the shop and ask for a bottle of 'orse oil. He also used to sell seeds, Carters seeds. *Ken Hyde*

If anything went wrong with the harness we had to go down to Mr Hyde in Regent Street, he had this little leather shop. He would make anything in the leather line you wanted, in fact, in the latter, years my father had two satchels made for both my sons and one is still used today as a tool bag, so that shows you how well made

---

* Propping up a group of sheaves.

they were. He used to repair the things for the harness such as the collars for the horses and also he'd mend the canvasses for the horse drawn-binders which used to cut the corn and bind it into sheaves. *Claude Ingrey*

Bruce Pateman, Slaughterhouse

A familiar sight to me was seeing a thousand pigs brought by droving along the road from Arlesey Station right to Pateman's slaughterhouse along High Street, and they used to load the carcasses into a big lorry out in the road. It was Ward & Sons, Smithfield market. *Claude Ingrey*

My father used to work at Pateman's slaughterhouse. They reckoned they used to kill about a thousand animals a week. At one time Banger Jeff did it. They used to have a mallet and he would stun the animal with this thing on the back of the neck, and before they had a chance to recover they would put them up on the pulley and just slit their throats. After that they had these big electric shears. We used to go and get lights and liver for dad to make faggots, and we'd sometimes have a pig's head on the table for a meal.

You'd walk along High Street with your lights and liver on a hook, all the way down to Vaughan Road, dripping blood all the way. If you wanted to get your tomatoes on quick you'd go to the slaughterhouse and when they slit their throats you would stand

Owen Hyde standing outside Hayes' shop, Regent Street.

there with a wide-necked bottle and collect the blood for the tomato plants, it was used as a fertiliser. *Alan Dear*

Bruce Pateman used to have 20 men or more working for him. At Christmas-time, on a quiet frosty night, you could hear them singing carols all over the village. They'd be working away and singing, it was lovely to hear them. They wouldn't start work till nine or ten o'clock at night and they would work through till they'd cleared all the animals. Alec Dean and Len Smith used to drive the lorries which went out to collect the pigs from various places. Bruce was a canny old chap, he'd fetch a crate or two of beer out, to keep them well oiled up. *Biffy Charles*

G Turner, Undertaker

Grandfather started his own building business in about 1880 with a man called Brockett. He also got into the undertaking business, it wasn't something you made a profit at, he used to do it purely to satisfy his customers. If you didn't do the undertaking for the family, well they took their lumber business somewhere else. In those days my grandfather used the parish hearse, the one you used to push. All the mourners used to walk. The average funeral at that time used to cost about nine quid, people couldn't afford any more.

When grandfather first started he lived in Regent Street, not far from where the Post Office is now, and he had a workshop at the top of the garden. Then grandfather built a house on the High Street for his brother-in-law, but he couldn't afford to pay for it so my grand-father had to mortgage it and live in it himself. We went to live there and father joined the business, they had their own workshop at the back where they used to make the coffins. They mostly got the coffin boards from Shepherd's.

Instead of headstones, which people couldn't afford, they had burial boards. It used to go long ways, the length of the grave, a board about nine or eleven inches wide, and they used to have a post each end which would be put in the ground. They were mostly painted white and they would write all the particulars in black on the side. No burial boards survive in this village today.

A lot of people were buried by the parish under the Poor Law and we used to be paid four quid. The only thing they wouldn't pay for was inside lining and they wouldn't pay for any furnishing on the outside or any mouldings. We used to bury people from the Three Counties and I remember they had a meeting and decided to stop a further three shillings because you hadn't got to put a pillow in.

When a person died, if you were Church of England you rung the knell at the church, but if you were a non-conformist they rung the bell at the cemetery. When Eustace Ginn used to ring the bell, he was supposed to ring it for twenty minutes, then they eventually cut that out.

Owen Hyde at work.

At one time when you took the coffins home it was unheard of to do this in the daytime, you had to wait until it was dark. Of course, there were no street lights and you weren't supposed to be seen. In those days there were no chapels of rest; people used to keep the bodies at home in their front rooms. We used to push the coffins about the village on a truck. When I was a little kid I used to go as well, I had to carry a lamp because there was no lights. We used to go down The Green a fair bit and old Kingy, who lived in Tythe cottage, put in a complaint. He said, 'We always know when Turner's truck's going by at night because we can sit here and hear it, and it's very disconcerting, very upsetting, to sit indoors and hear this coffin going by'. He made an official complaint, it caused quite a stir. So my grandfather had to take the wheels off the damn truck, take them to Baldock station and send them to

London, and have some rubber tyres put on, so that Kingy couldn't hear it. *George Turner*

When my mother died down here and Dad and Aunt Em was there, I had to go up the road at half-past-one in the night, and you were never nervous. I got Carrie Gentle and Selena Bass from Dines Row and they were the two women who used to have to come and lay these dead people out. I got up in the middle of the night and got them out of bed to come, and I was only a girl. *Maud Castle née Seymour*

A rather morbid subject, funerals, they used to ring the cemetery bell, it was one for a man, two for a woman and three for a child. They used to have a hearse on wheels which was pulled along. I can remember my brother's funeral in 1926. There was the flu epidemic, we all went down with this flu and he died I can remember the coffin being in our house, it was quite an experience for a young lad of eight. *Claude Ingrey*

Castle's Coaches

Castle's and the Stotfolder did a lot of good for this village. He'd run trips to Baldock fair, starting at about eight o'clock at night, backwards and forwards, and the last coach would be at a certain time. Originally the pie shop was built for Castle's coaches. I think Castle started off working for Pateman doing his cartage and he bought a Baco Ford for carting pigs, and then somebody took over from London and Castle went on to coaches. *Biffy Charles*

George Castle used the Stotfolder to take the football team to their matches. But before that he had an old lorry. He used to take the pigs to Bedford market in the morning, come back to the Chequers. Frank Brown and Len Smith used to scrub that out and they would put a couple of forms in. George Castle would come out with us, we'd go in the pub after a game, he'd have seven or eight pints and would bring us home as right as rain. *Alf Cardell*

Geoff Lamming, Milkman

Before I went to school, Lammings had the farm at Astwick, then Blacklers and then Struthers. Geoff Lamming used to go round with the milk cart and he used to pick me up and take me around on Saturday mornings. They used to milk down there and it was put into milk churns. Every night they used to go to Arlesey station to put the churns on the train for London or somewhere. *Maud Castle née Seymour*

John Oliver, Milkman

My father, John Oliver, was a milkman for 32 years and I used to do a milk round, I done it for 18 years. When we were short of milk we always went to George Saunders at The Poplars for extra milk. We kept our cows at Yew Tree House at the back. I was only 14 when I left school and I started helping my father straight away. I used to be fed up on Monday's because we used to have to go carting a lot of washing, my mum used to take in washing. Then she would send me back with it on Friday. I used to be on the milk round by eight every morning. We delivered twice a day, in the afternoons as well. I used to go right up to Arlesey Road, down Brook Street, Hitchin Road and part of Vaughan Road. I delivered it all on foot, going back and forwards fetching another hand-can and dipping it out. The can held about a gallon-and-half, something like that. We only made thruppence on a pint of milk. We used to make butter and cream to sell. *Olive Chapman née Oliver*

George Saunders, Milkman (and Farmer)

George Saunders from The Poplars used to come round on a bicycle with the milk, and when we first moved to Stotfold in 1927 I had orders to stand outside and not to move until I saw a man with a can on his bike, then I had to say to him, 'Please Mr Sanders will you call round'. *Claude Ingrey*

Teddy Dear, Coalman

Teddy Dear – he was a turn – he used to fetch coal from Arlesey to Stotfold. He had a bad stammer. Someone asked him the way to

An outing in one of Castle's charabancs, George Castle in the driving seat.

to Shefford once. He was telling them, 'U-u-p-p t-t-there, t-t-turn' and all this, and at the finish he said, 'B-b-ugger o-off, you'll be there before I can t-t-ell you'. And yet he'd get up and sing a song at these concerts and it was a pleasure to listen to him. If Teddy was singing you could guarantee a lot of people would be there. He's sung in the Liberal Club, Conservative Club, and the 'Tin Box'. *Biffy Charles*

Teddy Dear used to go and see old Mrs File, Bill File's mother down the Avenue. He also run a book on the quiet, and old Mrs File liked her tanner bet, she loved her tanner bet on the gee-gees. He went down there one week, with his coal cart like, went in the 'ouse and said 'yo-yo-you've g-g-got your b-b-loody coal for n-n-nothing again this w-w-eek'. Her bet had come up again. *Sam Pooley*

When I was a young lad I went in there once, because somebody had give me a hot tip, well I'd only got sixpence. So I said to Mr Dear, 'I want to back 'orse please. 'Wha-wha-what do you want t-t-o do then?' I said 'I want thruppence each way on this 'orse'. I think it came in third at about two-to-one on, and I had the cheek to go back to get my winnings. 'I backed 'orse this morning Mr Dear and it come in third, how much have I got to come back?' I got a penny, I think that was out of sympathy. *Edward Bowskill*

Reg Saunders, Fishmonger

I had the fish shop down Queen Street for two years or so just before the war, but it wasn't all that clever so I packed it up. After I'd completed my war service I came out and bought my first mobile, an old Morris Commercial 13-cwt. I did much better doing things that way, travelling round the villages. If we were short of money we could go and pick up a pound or two, but being stuck in a shop you'd got to wait for somebody to bring it to you. Eventually I got involved with Thurstons and did the fairgrounds, they helped me on quite a lot. I travelled with them for about 35 years, no messing we went all over the place from March until October. *Reg Saunders*

My dad was a soldier in the First World War and this particular night we'd got this fish and I said, 'Where did this come from?' 'Well', he said, 'Reg Saunders has come home from the war and he's set up this business and it's up to us to patronise him. He's been and done his duty and it's up to us to help him get going'. So Reg was a regular visitor to the house, selling my mum fish. So come the day I weren't well I was at home off work, that was how I met him, fish in hand, and that was it. *Hilary Saunders née Devereux*

Wren's, Fishmonger

Between the two World Wars, once a week the horse and cart of

Wren's the fishmonger of Biggleswade went round Stotfold selling fish driven by one of Mr Wren's tradesmen, Mr Redman. He was a fairly plump gentleman and wore a hard bowler hat, a blue suit covered by a smock and a whitish apron. There were all the usual fish: haddock, kippers, winkles, cod and sprats, etc. These were in small shallow wooden boxes on an open light-sprung cart. As he went along, he advertised his wares with a wonderfully penetrating cry which sounded like 'Cot-e-yar-mac', and then he would add in a lower voice as if to himself, 'Kipper, 'addock or cod, lady'. The one cry was invariably followed by the other. What 'cot-e-yar-mac' meant precisely is anybody's guess, though obviously it had something to do with cod and Yarmouth mackerel. Stotfold has not been the same since Mr Redman ceased to come round. *Bert Hyde*

Charley Loveridge, Rag-and-bone man

There were a lot of Loveridges, they were gypsies. There was Charley, he was a sergeant in the army, he was very well liked. They never caused any trouble or anything, they sold pegs and stuff and they used to do the rag and bones, and they used to come round with windmills, for a jam jar they would give you a windmill. *Alf Cardell*

Charley Dellar, Green-grocer

Everybody at that time used to have hens up the back garden, and when they had finished laying old Charley Dellar used to buy them

Left: The Stotfolder charabanc.

Right: Invoice for transporting the Rovers to away matches.

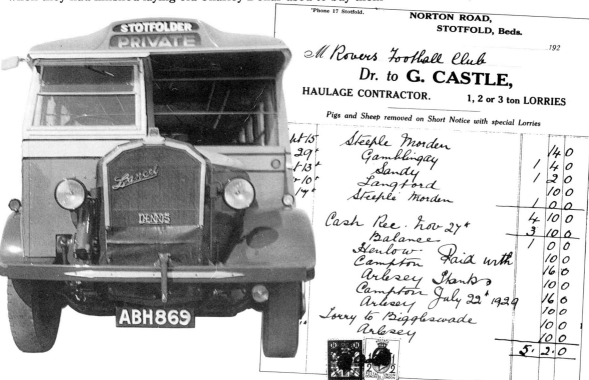

Mr Frank Cooper, Greengrocer, with his son Frank and wife, on the cart in Church Road, c. 1932.

to buy them for a few coppers. He would sit on his cart and pluck the feathers off these hens, you always knew when he had been along the road because there was a trail of feathers behind him. They were boiling hens, you had to boil them otherwise you couldn't eat them, they were tough. I think he sold them for about a shilling. He'd always got rabbits and hares as well. *George Turner*

Charley Dellar used to come and he'd bring rabbits. Well, me and my mate Fred used to go up the White Horse, take a pole with us and put 16 or 17 rabbits on this pole and take them round the village and sell them for a shilling each. We'd take these rabbits off Charley and he'd give us so much for selling them. We used to go to Radwell and gather watercress and take it round as well and sell it for a penny a bunch. *Alf Cardell*

The Whitening Man

There was a fella' from Baldock, I don't remember his name, but he used to come along with a horse and trolley, every Saturday morning selling balls of whitening. I think they were ha'penny a ball. The women used to buy them and every Saturday evening, especially in the summertime they used to whiten the front step, so that it was all spick and span ready for Sunday. If you walked down Dark Lane on a Saturday night you would see all these whitened doorsteps. They really stood out along there with all those tall dark trees. He used to go to the Lion works at Walsworth and buy the big lumps of chalk. That was his job on Monday morning and then he used to sit on the trolley on his way back to Baldock and he had a chopper and would fashion these balls as he sat on the cart. If you went from Walsworth to Baldock on a Monday afternoon there was this line of chalk chippings. People didn't take a lot of notice in those days because the roads weren't tarmacked, it was all stones. In the majority of the roads the grass grew up the middle. Then he used to go round the village on different days. *George Turner*

The Muffin Man

The muffin man used to come every Saturday afternoon, he used to walk from Letchworth with a tray on his head with muffins on and he would walk along and ring his bell. *George Turner*

Various Services

As well as the traders, there were many other colourful characters working within the community.

William Ingrey, Refuse Collector

My father opened a gravel pit along Arlesey Road in the 1920s, he used to supply to Redhouse, the builder, with gravel from this pit, but he had to close it in 1926 because Eames and Co. started up at Henlow with the lorries, and they could do it that much cheaper. In the late 30s Stotfold had no refuse collection so they wanted somebody to collect bottles, ashes and tins only, so my father thought he might as well fill up the gravel pit. He used to go round with a horse and cart two days per month to collect these things at each house. He had a big bath that he put all these things in before carting them off to the gravel pit. When the pit was nearly full to the top, we used to go to the cemetery and collect the surplus clay from the grave-digging and put that on top to help keep the moisture in, it's still along there today. *Claude Ingrey*

Julius Millard, Postman

He was the first postman I knew, he lived down Church Road. He would come round with the post. That would fluctuate, sometimes it would be an Arlesey address, sometimes Baldock, it went back and forwards several times. I think he used to have to go to Arlesey to fetch his letters. He'd got a whistle and when he'd delivered the letters in one area he would stop at each cross roads. He would stop at the top of Queen Street and blow his whistle and if you wanted any stamps you used to go out and he would sell them to you.

After him they changed it to Baldock and we didn't have our own postman, the Baldock one used to do it. First of all he used to bring all the letters for Stotfold on his bike, he would leave Baldock at about half-past-five in the morning and call at Radwell and deliver their post, then he'd deliver all round Stotfold. He'd be finished by eight o'clock. Well, opposite Bigg's butcher shop there was a field with a tin shed set up by the GPO. He used to go in there and cook his breakfast, they'd got a little combustion stove in there. Then at nine o'clock he used to go back round the village and empty all the post boxes and take the post back to Baldock. After that, when the post got a bit too heavy, they supplied him with a horse and cart. *George Turner*

Stotfold Memories

Wally the postman was out early each morn,
He'd collected the post from Arlesey, by dawn,
After sorting them, 'twas time for his round to begin,
Which included Whip Jacks, and also New Inn,
Both these places being well out of his way,
Sometimes their letters on Wally's mantelpiece would stay,
Only a ha'penny stamp, Johnny Dilley won't want that,
Nor Sunday's circular lying on his mat,
Unexpected, one morn, as Wally started his round,
The inspector was waiting, to time him, he found,
This unexpected pleasure perturbed Wally somewhat,
For letters for Whip Jacks he just had not got,
'I have been up a long time, I am feeling the strain,'
Wally offered the inspector tea, as they passed his domain,
The inspector sipped his tea, Wally approached the shelf,
Slipped the letters from Whip Jacks in his bag with stealth,
Johnny Dilley got a mat full of letters pushed in,
As did Arthur Castle and Will Green of New Inn,
The inspector was satisfied, Wally got his extra pay,
And congratulated himself on having a good day,
Wally finished his round, and changed his attire,
He wore his straw hat, and sucked his black briar.
With his drainpipe trousers, and black dickey bow,
With his cane on his arm, to the Black Lion did go,
The cane had a pin in the end beneath

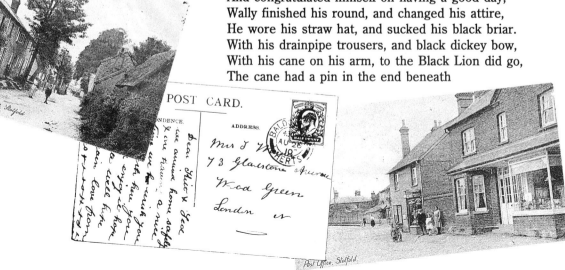

POST CARD.

Post Office, Stotfold.

Which he used to pick hops from between his teeth,
He flourished his cane as if striking a blow,
To encourage those present to vote for Prothero,
As the cane came to rest, Wally gave a grin,
For a packet of Woodbines was stuck on the pin,
Willie Bigg came in, and said thereupon,
Wally, how long has this been going on,
They made their peace, Wally borrowed a pound,
Then left for the Chequers, to buy a round.

Tempus Fugit

Harold Pooley, Road Repairer

We had a nice fella' Harold Pooley who used to be the village road
repair man, in fact my father used to contract a horse and cart to
the council a few days a month to go round and repair these pot
holes in the road. You'd have the horse and cart with the tarmac on
top and we'd be towing this brazier thing on wheels which had a
fire on, and we had a big bath on top in which you melted the tar.
Claude Ingrey

The Town Crier

There was also a Town Crier, the one I remember was a fella'
called Brown, I don't know what family of Brown's he come from.
When we lived in Queen Street, in the early 1920s, he used to
come along and ring his bell and stand in the middle of the hill they
used to call that Blacksmith's Hill at the time, because there was
always a blacksmith shop at the top of Queen Street. About the
only time that I remember seeing him was once or twice a year
telling people what time they had got to be at the 'Tin Box' to pay
their allotment rent. Whether he delivered any other messages or
not I don't know. *George Turner*

Mrs Patrick, Fortune teller

Mrs Patrick, the fortune teller, she was real. I never had mine told
by her, but Lil a pal of mine did, she was Kitchener's milk girl, at
the time. When she came back she told me Mrs Patrick had said
that she would be a widow by Christmas. She didn't get on too well
with her husband, so I don't think she was very worried. They left
here and went to Harringay, her husband's family had an ice-cream
business there. She wrote to me that Christmas and I wrote back
and put on my card, 'What about the widow's weeds?' Then she
wrote back and said, 'Burying Albert on Wednesday'. I know lots of
things she said came true. *Doll Howard née Westrope*

Chapter 8

Time Off

Both the Girl Guides and Scouts were popular with the youngsters of the village, the girls particularly enjoying camping and croquet on Ivy Ray's law. The Scouts had their meetings at Bury Farm, and Scoutmaster John Bigg bought the first uniforms for the troup.

There were groups and societies, too, for older members of the community to join: the Workers' Educational Association, the Stotfold Silver Band, the String Orchestra, Meccano Club, British Legion, and Army and Sea Cadets.

The Women's Institute also played a very important part in village life, ever since its foundation in 1933. Many women willingly gave their time to making it such a success, and Mrs Lizzie Pateman is particularly remembered for her 20 years' service as president.

Memories of Stotfold Silver Band

The silver band in splendour, in uniforms with braid,
The cart took them to Baldock, at the flower show they played,
They viewed the bandstand with disdain,
And sent for the secretary to complain,
We are too far from the beer tent, we've had enough of it.
You will either move us closer, or we'll all go down to the Vic.
When the overtures were finished, and the beer had ceased to flow,
Cyril got the cart out, and they prepared to go.
He led the horse between the shafts, and made the harness tight,
Then found the horse was back to front, and tried to put things right.
He tied the reins to the marquee pole, and the wantee to the wheel.
When the poor horse moved, the tent came down, and the cart did a Scottish reel.
When willing hands had put things to right, with the cart now in the stern.
The band climbed in with their instruments, and made for the weigh bridge turn,

Stotfold Silver Band c. 1914.

They turned the corner safely, and all cried with relief,
We are on the home straight now, and cannot come to grief.
The wheel caught in a culvert, with Cyril's hand unsteady,
And the band all left the cart, before they were quite ready.
'Twas such a predicament, that no one could foresee,
One with an oompah stuck on his head, and a trombone around
    his knee.
Someone stuck his head through the drum and Ted nearly had a
    fit,
If I could find my drumstick, what would I do with it!
The horse then bolted home, without its heavy load,
And the band played 'Come and join us' from a ditch in Baldock
    Road.

Tempus Fugit

The Cinema

Contrary to popular belief, the Regent was not Stotfold's first cinema. In 1910 a silent movie show came to the Pig and Whistle meadow, and from 1925 onwards Mr Aston Ayers from Ashwell showed silent films once a week in the Liberal Club in the High Street. This was always popular as a visit to the cinema was considered to be the highlight of the week.

A travelling silent movie show came to Stotfold in the Pig and Whistle meadow on the very spot where Hallworth House now

stands. During the interval of the movie film, the owner's daughter would sing the song that was written about the mine disaster that had occurred in 1910.

> Don't go down in the mine, Dad, dreams very often come true,
> Daddy you know it will break my heart if anything happens to you.
> Just go and tell my dream to your mates, it's true as the stars that shine,
> Something is going to happen today, dear daddy don't go down the mine.

Bert Jeffs

There was precious little in the way of entertainment in the village, occasionally a mobile cinema would come, and it would park in what is now the Liberal Club. They used to obviously show it from the outside, I don't know how it worked, because at the time I was only a kid. It cost about a penny for a show, which we thought was marvellous. *Doug Flitton*

The Regent Cinema

Frank Smith opened the Regent Cinema in a converted warehouse in Regent Street on 11 November 1929. It had seating for about 300, and proved to be such a popular venture that the Smith family decided to have a purpose-built cinema erected. The Regent Cinema, Arlesey Road, was opened on 15 April 1938 and ten years later was sold to Central Cinema (South Norwood) Limited who continued running it

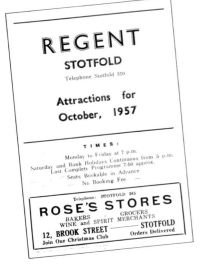

Top: Regent Cinema, Arlesey Road, 1950.

until May, 1952. Seating about 700 people, it cost £12,000 to build, and had a fully equipped stage, orchestra pit and Wurlitzer organ. During the war, the Pioneer Corps Orchestra from Radwell played on Sunday evenings. They also held inter-denominational thanksgiving services, with the Salvation Army band playing.

The Wurlitzer organ in the Regent Cinema.

When Reverend Crofts, the Baptist minister, was here, he started my father off with the cinema. He said that father would be the right man because he would show the right sort of films. We opened just a week or so before talking pictures came in. We had to show silent films until we got the right machines. *Bessie Upchurch née Smith*

I worked for the cinema for about 22 years. The cinema down Regent Street was in a very big old shed, didn't we do well! I used to go up there and work at the desk and issue tickets. That lasted for some time until they built the one along the Arlesey Road. They were good old days. The prices were 6d, 9d and 1s 3d. There was quite a lot of people who came to it. There was a lovely foyer thing and the desk was there. When we went to the new one, I was there the first day and I was there at the end.

When we were in Arlesey Road, Cramps went up there to live and the Dears, they used to store hundreds of bikes for tuppence a time. And these people that came from Arlesey, Henlow and Ashwell used to bike home from the pictures. *Maud Castle née Seymour*

I saw *Dracula* at the old cinema down Regent Street; it scared me to death and I ran all the way home. It was alright in Stotfold old cinema as long as it didn't rain hard, because the rain used to rattle on the roof. *Doll Gentle neé Peacock*

There used to be a cinema down Regent Street. I remember the seats were very, very narrow. We used to go with Mrs Empringham, the vicar's wife. She was very large, so we had to pick where we sat very carefully because some of the arms went up and she would overlap onto your seat. The cinema was a great treat. *Joan Smyth*

Harold Smith's father branched out and opened a cinema, that was a great asset. Harold Smith and I used to operate the equipment. When talkies first came out, you had a gramophone record for the sound, and you had to line the film up in the right position and then put the record dead on the arrow, so that when it all started up it was all synchronised otherwise the mouth was going and there was no sound or vice-versa. Eventually they improved on this and the sound track came on the film, and that was called, 'sound on film' and with that you couldn't go wrong. Later the cinema was built along Arlesey Road, and they had the organ installed. Harold Ramsey used to play the organ. There was another chap from Leamington Spa, I've forgotten his name, but he was rather a bumptious man. He pressed a switch and the organ rose up in front of the audience, then he played for 20 minutes, and then he pressed the switch for the organ to be lowered out of sight again. We were up in the operating box on one occasion and could see that he kept pressing this switch and nothing was happening. Fortunately Harold spotted it, and he rushed down and outside the cinema, right down to the inside where the organ was, and touched a lever which took the organ down. In the meantime, his father had come tearing up the stairs all hot under the collar because the chap couldn't get the organ to go down, but Harold had got it under control. *Doug Flitton*

Tennis players in Alex Smith's meadow, c. 1930s.

Sports

Stotfold had its fair share of sportsmen and women. The village had its own football and cricket teams, and tennis, bowls, darts and billiards were all well supported.

Football
Football in Stotfold has had a long and chequered history. The first game recorded in The Biggleswade Chronicle was in 1905 when Stotfold Reserves played Garden City, but football was certainly being played in the village long before that time.

There was always great rivalry between the village teams, Arlesey and Stotfold being no exception, and it was not unknown for matches in progress to be cancelled because of the excess of 'enthusiasm' this produced.

Football outing.

Many different team names have emerged over the years, for instance, Stotfold Athletic, Hornets, Rovers and Old Boys, who used various pitches: Cook's meadow, Smith's meadow, The Green, Smyth's meadow, Hitchin Road Recreation Ground and Northern's across the A1.

Wally Larkin started a football team, I don't think that it was called the Rovers then, but it was the same gang that started the Rovers. When we first started the football team, I don't remember who came with me but we went round to people asking for money to help us. We goes down to Donny Kitchener, and asks him if he can help the football team. He said, 'My dear fella' I've got a football team of my own to keep', but he still gave us ten bob. Then we went to Cross at Radwell, the butler comes to the door and says, 'What can I do for you?' 'We've started a football team up in Stotfold and we've made Mr Cross vice-president'. Of course, we had to make Alex Smith president because that was his field we were going to play in. Mr Cross come out, he was a white-haired old man with a very red face, and he gave us ten bob.

We started playing football up the rec, that was the first year it was built up there. But the grass was too long, and I asked them to do something about it. So they fetched all these sheep down to feed off it, they drove them all through the village. *Alf Cardell*

I played football for Stotfold for 13 years, I got a couple of medals. We used to go to the Three Counties and play football to entertain the patients. There used to be about 1,000 there then. You used to have all the doors locked behind you when you went in and when you come out. We used the sports room which had a billiard table in it, as our changing room. They used to line the patients all along one side of the touch line and all up the other side and then the football match would start. If you scored, they went mad, dancing about, but if the attendants scored they would boo. *Jack Brown*

What proper football we played, we used to play down on The

Stotfold Old Boys' team.
Biggleswade and District League,
Div II, Cup winners 1932–33–34
seasons.

Ladies' football match between
Miss Pearson's Gym Class and the
Women's section of the British
Legion, May 1937. The Gym Class
won 6–0.

Stotfold cricket team. c. 1928.

Stotfold Social Club playing bowls at the back of Mrs Westrope's shop, Brook Street, on August Bank Holiday Monday, 1929.

Stotfold Darts League.

Stotfold Liberal Club Billiards team. Division II champions of the Biggleswade and District Billiards League, 1938–39.

Top left: The first scout group of Stotfold, 1919.

Top centre: Women's Institute Annual Garden Party held in Mrs Pateman's garden.

Top right: Molly Langford's School of Dancing, c. 1950.

Bottom left: The first outing to Whipsnade Park of the Old People's Club, pictured in front of the Tin Box.

Bottom centre: Girl Guides camping at Pavenham, c. 1925.

Bottom right: Children's Christmas Party, c. 1950.

Green, and the 'Top-enders' would play the 'Green-enders'. I'll never forget Harold Hardy, he used to pick the 'Top-enders' team. He said, 'We've got to play for the cup this week, I'll bring it with me'. When we got there we said, 'Where's this cup then Harold?' He pulled an egg cup out of his pocket done up in silver paper. Horace Howard used to be the head 'Green-ender'. *George Turner*

Cricket

It could be argued that with the demise of the cricket club in the 30s, Stotfold was never the same place again. Once the club no longer had the use of Ray's meadow, in the heart of the village, it soon went into decline, despite the fact that it had always been a very successful team.

We had one of the prettiest little cricket grounds in the district. The actual pitch was just in the middle of the field, a table was never laid as such. It was a successful cricket team. They won the cricket league lots of times. When Ray left, Turby took over and that was the finish of that, he started selling off the land. *Sam Pooley*

We had a real good cricket team, too. Alf Mays, wonderful player, and Jack Busby played in Ray's meadow. Lovely trees, underneath

these we used to take the children. When it come to batting, if they hit it through Jack Ray's window they got a pound for it. Alf Mays done it no end of times. George Saunders, he was wonderful, he used to get a big score every week. When it was hot we used to go under the chestnut trees. *Wally Larkins*

Stotfold Old Boys' Athletic Club

The Old Boys' Athletic Club used to meet in the school. Brimmicombe, Charley Keeper and a couple from Letchworth Boys' Club used to run it. They formed a couple of football teams: Stotfold Old Boys. There was Jack Brown, my brother Chelsea, Eric Bygrave, Bob Cooper, even old Scummer was in it, his old tummy used to go up and down. As well as the football we'd go out running, starting at the Boys' School up Baldock Road and round the top of the road, and down by Whip Jacks and back. That was one little run. Then we'd come back and have to do skipping and then some would put the gloves on. We also did wrestling and gymnastics, it was amazing what they did do. Freddy Caine, he wasn't a bad little boxer. I did a little bit of boxing at the Boys' Club. *Biffy Charles*

Below: Women's Institute Annual Garden Party, c. 1934.

The Pubs

In 1876, according to the Return for Public Houses, there were five, public houses and 14 licensed beer houses, including the Two Chimneys, now in Letchworth. The Bell at New Inn, where the Little Chef now is, had closed around 1870. These 20 pubs served a population of 1,777. Since then, nine houses have ceased trading; in some cases the buildings still stand: Queen's Head, 97 Arlesey Road; White Hart, 54 High Street; Peewit, 83 Astwick Road; Cricketers, 97 The Green; Jolly Butcher 49 The Green; but of the rest, only the site remains: Boot, 83 The Green; Plough, 1 Rook Tree Lane; White Swan, 36 High Street; White-Horse, 112–114 High Street and Sun, Elizabeth House, High Street.

The Chequers (Stotfold's oldest pub)

My father used to drink in the Chequers, he used to tell me about Lizzie and Nellie; they would never let any more than three men in the bar at any one time. I wrote a little verse about them: Moons ago in Stotfold, two maiden sisters called Nellie and Lizzie, were licensees of the Chequers which kept them very busy. But alas only three men at a time were allowed in the bar. Whispered Nellie to Lizzie, we'll keep them afar, because we want to remain plain misses. *Mary Sapsed neé Triplow*

If anybody got killed in an accident they would be taken to the Chequers, to an adjacent little building. They would lay them in there and put them in a coffin, and an inquest would take place. Danny Gentle was killed on a motorbike at the cross roads and the inquest was held at the Chequers. *Biffy Charles*

Chequer's darts team celebrating a win, late 1930s.

The White Horse

The first publican of the White Horse in 1829 was James Porter junior. It had been suggested that he would make a good witness for the prosecution in the riots of 1830. The White Horse received its licence under an Act which came into force in October 1830. Before that time it traded as a beer shop without a name and did not have a license. The then owner was Pryor's Brewery of Baldock, later to become Simpsons. A description of Pryor's beer in 1823 says that it was of 'superior body and flavour resembling London porter in a great degree'. So a really first-class pint was available at the White Horse, if only the labourers of the village could afford it. Farm workers' wages in Stotfold and most other places in those days were not enough to buy the necessities of life, let alone beer. No doubt some took the view that ale was one of the necessities of life, but one way or another some of them must have scraped together enough money to buy James Porter's beer otherwise he would have gone out of business, for none other than the lower orders frequented a beer house. For many years there always seems to have been a Porter at the White Horse. *Bert Hyde*

The White Horse public house, c. 1928. Reg Saunders in foreground.

Jimmy Husband, he was the first chap to bring evening papers into Stotfold, in the early 1920s. At that time he would get them from a wholesaler in the Wynd in Letchworth. Well, they used to include the football and racing results and he would bring a bundle back to Stotfold and sell them in the pubs. If he sold enough in the White

Horse he needn't go any further. Eventually everybody used to congregate at the White Horse to wait for the papers. There was no wireless or television then, so unless you had a newspaper you didn't know what the results were. I know I wasn't very old, because he used to come by singing and shouting and wake me up as he went home.

In them early days they used to lock up the drunks in the 'cage' down the bottom of Queen Street. There used to be an old lady who lived on her own, where Jim Woodhouse used to live. And when anyone was locked up in the cage she used to go and sit beside them for a bit of company, if it was fine, and talk to them all night. She used to make them a cup of tea, but she couldn't get a cup through the bars so she used to pour the tea pot down their mouths, by putting the spout through the bars. Then the police used to hire a horse and cart and take the offender down to Biggleswade next day. *George Turner*

I think my grandfather took over the White Horse in the early 1900s. Then it came to my uncle Cyril, but as he was single my mother, being his sister, decided the family should go and live with him. I done all my school days from there. The White Horse was a beer house in the early days, but eventually it did become fully licensed. They used to go down to the cellar and draw it out of the barrels in them days, no pumps. It was 4d a pint then and I had plenty at that price and all. Even when I was about eleven I would go down the cellar, shove the old jug under the tap and tip it on a little bit. Our beer came from Simpson's brewery. They used to have sing-songs in the pub, with the old piano and drums. That was good entertainment in them days. There were about four or five people who used to bring their own jugs for a fill up and then take their beer home to drink. Very few women drank in the pub, and if they did their beer was drawn from the barrel in an earthenware jug and they were given a glass so that they could pour the beer into the glass and drink in a more lady-like manner. *Reg Saunders*

The White Swan

I can remember the pub called The Swan; it was a low cottage with a thick thatch. When I was about seven years old, they had army manoeuvres in Stotfold, about 1912, and there were these soldiers with their horses standing outside this pub drinking beer. Anyway, my father bought the Swan and he had two houses built in its place which were called Swan Villas. *George Shepherd*

Wheelbarrows push up the hill

At the Black Lion public house, on a summer's day,
Fred Howard and Peter Smith had a few words to say.
The wagers were struck, after they had supp'd their fill,

The inn sign of the old Sun public house.

Peter was to push Fred, in a barrow, up Wilbury Hill.
As neither had a wheelbarrow to use, it would appear,
They adjourned to the White Horse, to consult with Jamie Dear.
Jamie's barrow was not for letting, for a wager as such,
It was needed to transport his customers, when they imbibed
    too much.
Eventually, as Peter had applied his usual charm,
A barrow was borrowed, from the farmer at Wilbury Farm.
At the Fuzzens, they all with one accord did gather,
Long Sid and Little Jack, agreed to profit from the matter.
With a barrel of Flitton's beer, and a few quart pots,
They set up a bar, amongst the forget-me-nots.
There was Piggy and Dabtoe, Little Hat and Chowney,
Taff, Gee and Lincoln, Skinny Jack and Brownie.
To mention but a few of the crowd that gathered there,
Adding to the excitement, and to see that things were fair.
As the big push started, on it's journey not to stop.
Things began to happen amongst the crowd left at the top,
Who could drink most beer, while the push was under way,
The winner taking the jackpot, was the order of the day.
Peter finished the climb, complete with Fred aboard,
And was cheered by all, in amazement and accord.
The crowd then left the Fuzzens, forget-me-nots and all,
Also the birds and bees and creatures, great and small,
The barrow was left behind, for what reason you suppose,
For the jackpot winner needed it, to lay in and repose!

Voltaire

The Cage, Queen Street, where the drunks were locked up for the night.

The Black Lion

The Black Lion, that was a rare pub that was, before the war they were the best times I had in there. The beer was J W Green's of Luton, the only Green's pub in the village at one time. That was a lovely pint of beer. If people weren't used to it and they came up the Black Lion for a couple of pints, they reckoned they used to be 'running' for a week.

There were some real characters who used to go in the Black Lion: Kelly Bygrave, Walt Reilly, Beaver, Ginger Gentle, Ephraim Dear. Ephraim used to work his guts out sowing soot for about a fortnight or so and then go out and spend it all on the booze, and he'd keep on the booze until the money had gone. Chubby Day, he used to sow the soot. They tell me, I don't know if this is true, but Mrs Day used to make Chubby sleep up the garden, to sleep it off. Then there was Jack Larkins and Sailor Bill.

There used to be a little old organ thing in there, you used to wind the handle up and you'd have to put a penny in to get it to play. There were some older lads, Miller and co, they was the clever boys. They put the penny with a bit of tape on it and a bit of string and they would put the penny in just far enough so that it would knock the thing down and then pull it out again, and they'd get the tune for nothing.

Mrs Rose used to play the piano and we would have a real old sing-song. Then Bill Phillips, he came along and his favourite was, 'How they tittered, how they laughed'. Another song was, 'Through the old church door I hear an organ playing, through the old church door I saw the parson praying'. 'And the smoke blew up the chimney just the same' – every song used to finish with that. New Year's Eve, that used to be quite a do. 'I see the old faces and places I knew, I listen with joy, as I did when a boy, to the sound of the old village bell. The light was burning brightly, banishing all troubles and care, and the bells was ringing the old year out and the new year in'. Black Lion choir they used to call it. *Biffy Charles*

Ted Jones who worked at Coleman's, he lived opposite the Black Lion and he used to cut hair at his house. Anyway they all used to go to the 'waiting room' in the Black Lion and when the person finished having his hair cut, he would go back to the pub and shout, 'next'. *Gordon Huckle*

The Jolly Butcher

The Jolly Butcher was named after Cordie Shepherd's father who ran the pub. (The pub was granted its license in 1867, it was formerly called Dilley's Beer House). It was a Simpson's pub. I know a lot of people used to call it the Dust Hole. I just want to put the record straight – the name came about because there used to

Above: The Black Lion public house, c. 1916.

Right: The Jolly Butcher on The Green was in the thatched cottage in the centre of the picture.

be a dust heap, a big hole in the ground, at the side of the building where everybody came and dumped their rubbish, not because the pub was a dusty place. *Phyllis King née Brown*

The Pig and Whistle

During holiday time they used to play quoits down the Pig and Whistle and they'd be there drinking beer all day long, and throw a quoit just the same at the finish. They must have drunk 30 pints and still walk as right as rain. They were round steel rings they threw, nearest to the sticks. They could throw these quoits too, Jo Cox and them. We used to go down there and watch them. *Alf Cardell*

I remember Ambrose when he kept the Pig and Whistle, and it was busy one night and he said, 'Why the bloody hell they all come here, I don't know'. That was a real old village pub.

There was an old boy, Sam Hewitt, who lived along Dark Lane. He'd go out ferreting and netting rabbits and that sort of thing, then he'd go in the pub with a sack full of these rabbits and they used to buy 'em a tanner a time. Plus he'd get tuppence for a skin from the rag and bone men. *Sam Pooley*

My first wife, Ivy, she used to play the piano, she could play anything, mate, she was lovely. When I first met her she was playing in the Pig and Whistle, Bertie Coates kept it then. When she was at the Pig, Ben Robinson would write a list of tunes to play and he would play the drums. She also played at the Coach and Horses. Harry Dobson and them used to be down there then. They used to sing, 'The old church door'. She would only play Saturday and Sunday nights. Every Sunday we used to get the News of the World and in there was a sheet of paper that had music on it, she would always play it. *George Shepherd*

The Crown

We went into the Crown in January 1939 and we came out in January 1955 when my father retired. The beer was Wells and Winch, the pub was always full up. During the war we closed three or four days a week because we would sell out of beer. It was terrible during the Feast we were so busy. *Mary Westrop née Pearmain*

Finch Gentle's missus, Carrie, I was talking to her once and she said that Finchey had been having a late session in the Crown one afternoon. She'd got the dinner ready, put it on a place and walked it across to the Crown and said, 'There y'are have it while it's warm'. Carrie was a case she was. *Sam Pooley*

Below: The Crown, The Green, with the pond in the foreground.

Chapter 9

To Church on Sundays

Sunday Worship

Sunday was always a special day, when work was put aside and people put on their best clothes to attend their place of worship. The church and chapels were the cornerstone of village life. Until 1910 all the girls in the village had to curtsey to the Vicar, not only when they saw him in school but also if they passed him in the village, otherwise they got into trouble at school. This did not 'sit' too well with the parents from the large section of the population who were non-conformists.

Sunday was a different day entirely, you used to clean the shoes of a Saturday night ready for Sunday service, you never cleaned shoes on Sunday or did any sewing. As the legend goes, adjacent to us at Radwell, a person there was sewing in the church on a Sunday, pricked her finger and died.

They used to give away bread at one time to the poor of the parish. If you went to church Sunday morning you could get the bread but you had to wait until 12 o'clock.

Eustace Ginn used to ring our three heavy bells. It was John Holding, the vicar, who gave the clock and all that. When people heard these three bells rung they used to sing, John Hol-ding, John Hol-ding, to the ringing of the bells. Those three bells, one weighed a ton and half, the second one weighed a ton and the third weighed half a ton. Eustace used to ring them on his own. He had to get one going and keep that going, then he got the next one going. He'd do one with each hand and then he got the centre one going and controlled that with his foot. And he rung the three like that. *Claude Howard*

Eustace

Eustace was a man most versatile,
Did other jobs for quite a while.

Top right: Church Road with St Mary's Church in the background.

Bottom right: St Mary's Church choir, c. 1928.

As was his wont, he tolled the knell,
To assist one to Heaven, or down to Hell.
He played the organ at St Mary's Church
And often for a blower had to search,

At weddings and funerals he liked to be,
For the opportunity to charge a fee.
Church clerk, sexton, choirmaster too,
For Empringham he had much to do.
From church to grave he led the bier,
Carrying the cross for all to fear.
With his black skull cap, and his surplus short,
Trimmed with lace, his wife had bought.
Looking over his specs with thin, gold frame,
He would sprinkle the earth where you were lain.
With the dominoes at the Chequer's Inn,
He rarely played without a win.
Randall, Millard, Tinker and Rowley,
He beat them all, but sometimes slowly,
He rode his bike at a very slow rate,
Or walked, with his own particular gait,
Our blacksmith was of stature slight,
One wonders where he found his might.
Never raised his voice, but had his say.
As he travelled life, in an unhurried way,
No man of substance, no means to plan,
But a fine old English, gentleman.

Tempus Fugit

Sunday was church, we went to St Mary's very regularly. The first time Daddy took me to church alone, I was wearing my straw hat with the elastic under the chin, and I kept pulling mine because it was too tight and suddenly the elastic broke and my hat shot over two pews. When we got home Daddy said, 'I'm never taking that child to church again'. *Ina Roberts née Smyth*

I put a peppermint in the plate one day. We were always given a penny to put in the bag, and one day I exchanged my penny for an extra strong peppermint. And when we got out into the porch, Daddy put his hand out and said, 'Now, Joan, I will have your penny'. I can remember the awful feeling now, at how wicked I'd been. I sewed a button on once on Sunday and Daddy found me. He said, 'You know if you prick your finger you'll die after it'. *Joan Smyth*

In the churchyard at Astwick, they've got a vault there. If the moon was shining you would see figures going round the vault, I've seen it myself. My toilet used to be outside the house and it backed onto the churchyard. Joe's mum came to visit and I said, 'Don't go out there, because at 12 o'clock at night you'll see them going round the vault'. 'I won't see anything,' she said, but she did. We used to see it when the moon shone on that sundial on the front of Astwick Church. That was the only thing that frightened me. *Peg Humphries née Millard*

The Salvation Army Band.

We used to be naughty boys at Harvest Festival in the Salvation Army hall. People used to give vegetables and they'd be sold on the Monday. We'd sit up at the back of the hall and they used to bid for the produce. Well, we'd bid a bit, then it would go a bit higher, and then, when it came to the top price and stopped, we hadn't got the money to pay for it, so we were thrown out. An old lady, Bessie Payne, she always used to go to the Salvation Army at night when she was drunk and they used to turn her out because she used to make a nuisance of herself. *Jack Brown*

The Salvation Army used to have their meeting at the corner of Coppice Mead and offerings were taken at the conclusion of the meeting. The drum was laid on its side and the coin offerings were thrown onto the drum. I can remember causing a little bit of amusement for the spectators on one Sunday evening by falling into the brook in my Sunday-best 'Norfolk' jacket suit. *Bert Jeffs*

We used to have an open-air meeting every Sunday night at the top of the Avenue, and we marched right down the Avenue and down Regent Street to the old hall. In the winter we had a lamp. We used to play three marches then we would stop and play on the Crown corner near the pond. Lots of people used to come out and see the band.

A man named Joe Payne, he lived in Rose Cottage in Brook Street and worked on the land, he'd only got one pair of boots. He was cleaning his boots one Saturday night and the clock struck 12,

Top: Hope Chapel, Queen Street, c. 1920. Olive Chapman in the foreground.

Middle: Interior of the Wesleyan Chapel, High Street.

Bottom: Centenary celebrations of the founding of the Primitive Methodist Chapel, Brook Street, 1945.

well he'd cleaned one but the other was still dirty. So he had to go to chapel with one dirty boot and one clean one.

Benny Morris lived in Dark Lane, he used to come out of the pub Sunday afternoon and go into chapel with grandfather Scott and he'd sit and go to sleep, and start snoring. My grandfather used to dig him in the ribs with his elbows to wake him. When the snoring got too bad they took him out.

I played trombone for 43 years for the Army, I joined when I was 21. I only had two or three lessons, I picked it up as I went along. Some of the instruments came from the Silver Band. When it broke up, Bruce Patemen sent his men along to the White Horse, (that's where they used to practise) to collect these instruments to take them to his house, and they all came along playing these here instruments. They had to pay him £145 for the instruments. I had one of the trombones. The one I played is still in use today. *Albert Scott*

I had to go to the Salvation Army, mother was in the Army. I hated the Sunday School. I had a pair of shoes that had a bar across which was secured by a button. Well one Sunday the button came off and I had to walk all the way to Sunday School dragging my foot along, because it was wicked to sew a button on. *Lily Edmonds née Huckle*

In the days before electric motors, church organs were pumped manually. When I was a boy in the late 1920s I was organ blower at the Old Baptist Chapel. I sat in a cubby hole by the side of the organ which stood in the front of the chapel, being hidden from the view of the congregation by a red curtain. This had its advantages. However, it was also next to the pulpit under the immediate eye of the preacher, which was not so good. My predecessors in the job had been Doug Flitton, Harold Smith and Reg Brown. We had all scratched our initials beneath one another with a pin on the nicely varnished wood of the organ. There were other names too. The practice had started at an earlier date. The pay was three shillings a quarter. During the hymns, the voluntary, etc. I stood working a long wooden handle up and down to keep the organ supplied with wind. In the back of the organ was a large bellows, attached to which was a long cord. This cord ran through a small hole in the side of the organ; at the end was a small flat lead weight. This went up and down registering the amount of wind in the bellows. If it rose above a certain point the organ stopped. Sometimes on hot days I got tired and sleepy and let the wind get low so that the organ became silent. Realising in a flash what had happened I would begin pumping again as fast as I could. Of course, the whole congregation knew what had occurred; they had been left singing for a moment without the organ. Mr Frank Smith who owned the cinema was organist in my day. He was a wonderful musician, but without the organ blower he couldn't play a note. *Bert Hyde*

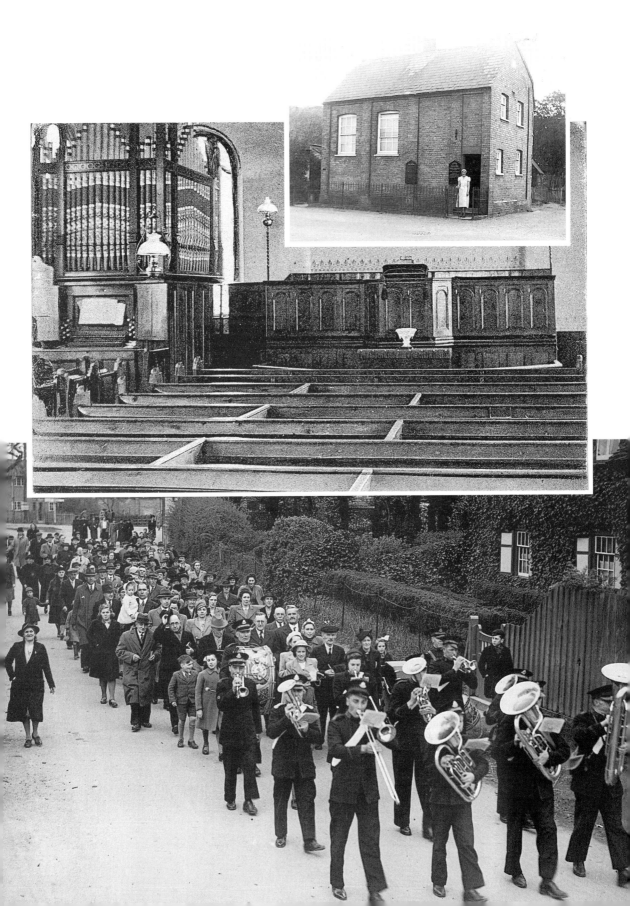

Sunday School treat for the children of the Baptist and Wesleyan Chapels, c. 1920. Held at the Bury, Astwick.

I went to the Wesleyan Methodist. I was a Sunday School teacher for quite a few years, and I was in the choir. I had a very good voice. I only sing hymns, nothing else. I was very involved with the chapel, they used to have something on there every night. Once I won a five shilling prize for reciting a poem. Mine was the best of the lot. I can still remember it now.

> You may go through the world but will be very slow
> If you listen to all that is said as you go.
> You'll be worried and fretted and kept in a stew,
> For meddlesome tongues must have something to do
> And people will talk.

Mill Dear neé Smith

My grandfather told me about Hope Chapel and how it started. There was a chap who played for the Rehoboth Chapel on Sundays, but during the week he played at the Chequers public house. So Mr Mehew, being pastor at the Rehoboth, had a meeting and said they couldn't have things like that. I think there was a bit of a row over it and Mr Mehew and some of the others picked up their things and left. Then he built our chapel, Hope Chapel. Grandfather was a minister and he had white fronts and collars which were all starched, and he went out from place to place preaching with a pony and trap. At the chapel my father started the singing for 32 years with a blow pipe (a small reed) that's still done today. *Olive Chapman neé Oliver*

Sunday Walks

The Old Baptist Chapel bible class, taken in Cook's meadow, c. 1920.

In the summer, during the 20s and early 30s, my brothers and I often used to go for a walk on a Sunday afternoon. Sometimes we would cross the smallholdings meadow, go over the Ford Bridge, along the Hullocks footpath or round Whip Jacks hill, down the Great North Road to New Inn. New Inn is the whole area around the Tudor Oaks and the Little Chef. At that time the old toll post, the Round House, which stood on the north side of the Hinxworth Road junction, sold sweets etc. even on a Sunday. But we did not normally go that far. Instead we turned down Taylor's Road, beside which runs the Cat Ditch. It was a fairly clear, fast-flowing stream in those days. We broke off short twigs or found short lengths of straw and threw them into the water, like A A Milne's 'Pooh sticks'. Then we had a race as we followed the progress of our own particular sticks, throwing stones at them if they happened to get lodged. This went on right up to the Limes which is just short of the point where the Cat Ditch flows into the River Ivel near Taylor's Mill bridge. The first one to the Limes, (now Ivel Mill House) won the race. Then, passing by Fen End, and perhaps pausing awhile to throw skimmers across the old pond, which was situated at the corner of the Green opposite the Crown public house, we made our way home. *Bert Hyde*

For Sunday walks we used to go along to the Baldock Road and through the six stiles. We used to cross over from the mill, across into the Bury meadow, which used to be full of snowdrops in the spring, then wander on by the Blue corner, across the Ford Bridge and on to the Splash, and then we'd go down to Golden corner, the Osier beds and then we'd stop at somewhere like Taylor's mill. *Gordon Huckle*

Church social life

As well as fulfilling a spiritual need, the churches and chapels were the main source of diversion, organising yearly outings – often to the seaside – fetes, bazaars and plays, which were always performed to enthusiastic audiences.

The Methodist Sunday school treats were in Mr and Mrs Blackler's field, they used to be the mainstay of the chapel. We used to get cowpats all over us, scrabbling for sweets. When we got fed up with going down there for our treat, we used to go to Skegness by train, and sometimes, when Castle's had the charabancs, we used to go in them to Clacton. *Mill Dear née Smith*

We used to have our Sunday School treats from the Wesleyan chapel down Blacklers, Astwick Road. We would have a tea, we had to take our own mug. Mr Levitt brought big tins of sweets, and we had to scramble for these sweets in the grass. Mill Dear was my

Salvation Army outing, in the Stotfolder, c. 1933.

Sunday School teacher. We would go down in Mr Blackler's horse and cart. *Edna Darton née Gentle*

When we had our Sunday School parties, Harris used to bring their galloping horses, and they used to have the field, you know where Roecroft is now, with a roundabout in it, and then we were given two blue tickets and you could have two rides. *Florence Phillips née Gentle*

I used to go to the Primitive Methodist Sunday School when I was a littl'un, especially when their outing was about due. The Prims used to hire one of these one-'orse coaches and go to Bedford and spend a day on the river. We used to have to get out and push it up 'ammer 'ill. *Archie Shepherd*

For our Sunday School treats we used to walk to Arlesey station and go on the train to Skegness. My mother had seven children and we all used to go. She used to take the bread as it was, wrapped in a cloth, the margarine, jam or whatever filling and a knife. Come lunch time, we all used to sit around Mum. She'd get the cloth out and cut bread. Each one in turn got a slice and by the time it was your turn again, you'd finished eating your first piece of bread. *Edward Bowskill*

I went in one of Watkins' buses in 1928 with a party from the Old Baptist Chapel, which used to be in Rook Tree Lane, to the tercentenary celebration of John Bunyan's birth at Elstow. *A W Watkins*

Salvation Army members visiting the seaside, 1937.

Bold Robin and the Babes,
performed by St Mary's Sunday
School, 1933.

of Biggleswade are still in business as agents for Vauxhalls. They had three charabancs named Pip, Squeak and Wilfred, which had some topical connotation which I have long since forgotten. *Bert Hyde*

One of the most successful events connected with the Stotfold Old Baptist Sunday School was the annual seaside outing. It was commenced about 1897 by Miss Annie Flitton assisted by her brother, Mr F C Flitton, and the teachers. The older children paid 2d per week and the juniors 1d per week from the first Sunday in January to the end of July. This amount was augmented by the proceeds of a concert and a few subscriptions from friends. It hardly seems possible that, for the small sum of 8s 6d seniors and 4s 3d juniors, the scholars and teachers could have travelled such long railway journeys to famous and distant seaside resorts.

What preparations there were to make! Miss Flitton made plain and currant cake. The men made gallons of lemonade at the brewery. It was quite a task to get 80 children and adults to Arlesey or Baldock stations. We had to appeal to friends to help us. Cheerfully they responded, brewer drays from Flittons, a pig float for the little ones from Mr Ingrey, spring carts, one drawn by a horse named Cobby, and a few solid-tyred bicycles.

So we all arrived at the station, and this before six o'clock in the morning. The train would draw into the station almost on time. Soon all were aboard for the long journey. After about two hours the cakes and lemonade were handed round. We generally arrived at the sea about 11 o'clock. The children quickly rushed to the beach where they played until four o'clock tea time. After tea at some restaurant, there was another hour-and-a-half play on the sand. At six o'clock they were rounded up for the station and home.

It was a tired but happy group that arrived back at Arlesey or Baldock station at midnight. Yes, the drays, the pig float, the spring carts and the bicycles were all there to convey them in procession on the last stage of the journey. Some of the places we went to were Clacton, Cromer, Grimsby, Portsmouth, Southsea, Southend, Dover, Skegness, Brighton and Scarborough.

Miss Bessie Smith (now Upchurch) continued to organise the Old Baptist Sunday School seaside outing until about 1933. *Written by Harry Hyde in 1956, reflecting on his memories of the Old Baptist Sunday School outings.*

Below: The Vicarage Fete, c. 1932. Left to right: Joan Smyth, Mrs Johnson, Mrs Smyth, Ina Smyth.

Chapter 10

Special Occasions

Hospital Day

Before the National Health Act of 1946, hospitals were run on a voluntary basis. In Stotfold, most people contributed 2d per family per week. In order to raise additional funds, a hospital 'demonstration' was arranged. The first one took place in 1914. Undoubtedly one of the highlights of village life, it was always arranged for the week preceding the Feast, originally on the Saturday. Then, in later years, it was held over two days with the Hospital Day and fete on the Saturday and an evening service on the Sunday. Some years after, the service was replaced with a concert which was held on a platform erected on the west side of The Green. A grand procession paraded round the village and then returned to The Green where side shows and competitions would be enjoyed by all.

Collecting for Hospital Day.

Saturday afternoon they used to have Hospital Day. Ever so big procession with two or three bands. Alex Smith used to ride right in front on a big white horse. Big banner, a huge banner in fact, you couldn't pass it if you come the other way. The procession went right round Rook Tree Lane, up Queen Street, down Brook Street, up the Folly, down Regent Street and into the meadow. *Wally Larkins*

Freddy Hyde, he always used to dress up. One year they were putting the sewer on, he wheeled a wheelbarrow round and dressed up as a navvy. One year he had the Crucian feeling. You know they used to have Crucian Salts and he was jumping up and down. *Albert Scott*

Grandfather always kept secret what he was going as for Hospital Day. People used to try and get out of him what his outfit was going to be. They would tease him by saying, 'I know what you're going to be this year, Freddy, a bloody fool, like you were last year'.

But one year Freddy really did fool everybody. It was when radio first came out, it was a real novelty. Anyway, he had this tent and he was charging people to come in and listen to the first radio, which he had in this tent. But what people didn't know, it wasn't a radio at all. He'd got an old sugar box and done it up to look like a radio. The sound, supposedly coming from the radio was in fact from a phonograph wound up round the back. Everyone had a good laugh about that. *John Hallworth*

Most years I used to try and do some sort of silly little thing, dress up as something. You used to hear talk about the old ploughing engines, steam engines. We done that one year, made out of four pram wheels and a tin body and we put a sack in it and let it smoulder and that made smoke come out of the chimney. We won a first prize for that. When we was coming up Queen Street on the way back, a blooming great big car pulled up and they gave us another couple of pounds. I think there were four of us, I can remember Teddy Levington and also Dick Bew. *Reg Saunders*

There was a Meccano Club in Stotfold. We built the Eiffel Tower out of Meccano and we had it on a truck and they pulled it round in one of the Hospital Days. It was seven or eight feet tall, and they put me on the truck to hold it. And walking behind was a chap with a trombone and as he played he kept poking the back of my leg. I didn't think much to that. *Albert Scott*

Parading around The Green, 1915.

Hospital Day, Stotfold, 1915.

Below: Mr Alex Smith leading the Hospital Day Parade, his son, Malcolm, dressed as a French officer, daughter, Olive, in highland dress, 1915.

Far left: Stotfold Fire Brigade, 1915, with a manual engine on loan from the Asylum.

Left: The Conservative Club's 'Britannia' float, Hospital Day.

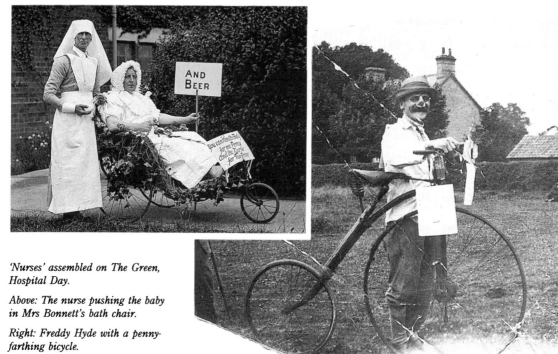

'Nurses' assembled on The Green, Hospital Day.

Above: The nurse pushing the baby in Mrs Bonnett's bath chair.

Right: Freddy Hyde with a penny-farthing bicycle.

Stotfold Feast

The Feast goes back a long way, but the exact date it started is not known. Originally it was held in the High Street, along both sides of the road, from the Black Lion right back as far as the Queen Street junction. It moved to its current location on The Green in about 1875. Every Stotfold person, and many more besides, visited the Feast every year. It was a great festival and was always held on the second Friday after the first Monday of July. The festivities ended with a Drumhead service on the Sunday, organised by the British Legion with the Salvation Army and Stotfold Silver Bands in attendance.

The best day in Stotfold fair was when they came in with horses, 18 to 20 horses on a big truck. Switch-backs, great big old trucks as long as two of these houses put together. There must have been 200 horses come in The Green during that week. *Wally Larkins*

I first came to Stotfold over 60 years ago, I was in show business. My first husband, Arthur Westrope, was older than me. He told me that they used to charge thruppence a wheel, so if you'd got a

A group of pierrots, representing the Liberal Club, Hospital Day, 1915.

caravan with four wheels it would be a snilling, and if you had two loads it would be two shillings. But after the machine people took it over it was so much a foot. Down the Coach end it was sixpence a foot, ninepence a foot in the centre and a shilling at the other end.

In the early days it was a big event, people used to come from all round the village to see the travellers pulling into The Green with all the horses. There used to be crowds there and it used to be the same when we were pulling out. We always travelled with the Harris family, and all their horses used to go down Blackler's. It used to be a shilling a night which would include feed.

The children's rides was a ha'penny and big rides a penny. The big rides were the galloping horses, chair-o-planes and the cake walk. And there used to be what we called the steam yachts, the boats used to go up and down. It had an engine in the middle. My brother had those, the dodgems and chair-o-planes. We travelled within the Eastern County section which covers this part; everyone had to belong to the Showman's Guild.

The wagons we had were all made of wood. We had little ranges in the wagons where we used to do our cooking. We also did our own washing. We had little hand washing machines that you pushed backwards and forwards, and we would have a little mangle we would screw onto a table outside. All my boys were born in the wagons at different places. George was born on the ground where Sainsbury's old shop used to be in Letchworth town centre, John at Potton and Miley was born at Biggleswade.

We could always get water on the fairground. We used to have a pony and trap, which we used to ride about to do the shopping and things like that. We always lent them our pony for fetching the water; they used to have a big barrel on wheels which they called a 'dandy' and that used to fetch the water back and forwards all night for the engine.

When I first came here I had to walk up Oliver's Lane right up to the Post Office, which was in the High Street. I used to think it was dreadful to have to walk up there and back. We used to have to get 'occasionals' for the tobacco licences because we used to use Player's cigarettes as prizes. We also gave all sorts of china and glass dishes, cups and saucers, everything in the way of china. We always got our stuff from a place in Petticoat Lane in London. I used to phone up and ask him to send us a case of 'swank' stuff, he knew what we wanted, about 12 dozen in a case.

I used to do the spit rock, the only ingredients I used was soft brown sugar and a little bit of butter. You had to boil it and then pull it. I made tons of the stuff for my rock stall. I always used to make it on The Green, in the open, so that people could see it being made. Although they called it spit rock you didn't spit on your hands as people thought, the rock was boiling hot, so you blew on your hands to cool them. To make the humbugs, you pull the white and you cool it, then you break so much off before you cool it and keep it warm, then you stretch your brown and put it round it.

I can remember seeing The Green up to your ankles in confetti. We used to sell a lot of water squibs and people would go round squibing each other. I've still got the pliers now that we used to screw them up with. I used to have a table with the confetti and squibs on. We used to send to London for the confetti, we would buy it in half hundredweights.

We knew everybody in Stotfold and everybody used to come and talk to us when we were open, it used to be lovely. Lots of places we went to we didn't know anybody. Billy Wood's had the boxing booth and my cousin used to have the Wall of Death. There was a dark man who walked on coals, danced on glass and ate fire, he called himself Prince Ambagasha; his name was really Barrett. He travelled with us all summer.

They used to keep open until one o'clock in the morning and it would always end up with a fight, Biffy and his brother Chelsea was always in it. *Doll Howard neé Westrope*

In the early 1900s when I was a young boy, they used to say, 'Are you coming to Stotfold Feast, old'un, and have two bites off one cherry', because it was cherry-time then, and they used to make cherry pies. It was a great do the Feast, I went with my aunt,

Admiral Beatty

Stanley Thurston's Gondolas, c. 1920.

everybody went. And my grandfather had a house party, they always had an enormous table loaded with food. *Cecil Edwards*

The large steam engines of the fair had an attraction all their own. They used to come puffing along with their huge rear wheels pulling up to three or four wagons. Stotfold Feast was a fairly large one so there were perhaps six engines in all. Those I remember were Admiral Beatty with the Thriller, Britannia bringing Thurston's Dodgems, Dreadnought with Jollity Farm, Surprise pulling Harris's Dodgems, the smaller Lord Lascelles brought Harris's roundabouts and Mannings big horses were hauled by Little Billie. The big horses used to be the main attraction in the early days. They had a centre piece with a steam driven engine. The organ was also in the centre. Every now and then the engine would give a piercing whistle, which would make those close by jump and could be heard all over the village. *Edward Hyde*

Having lived on this plot now for 70 years or so, I've seen a few Feasts come and go. In my boyhood days it was far more than it is now. It was a great meeting place; if people lived away they would return for the Feast and stay with relatives. This place was absolutely choc-a-block, it was all steam in those days, no lorries. The horses used to pull the caravans. As far as sanitation went I wouldn't like to say what happened actually. Down this meadow, when they came in July when it was hot, you'd see them flopped

Stanley Thurston's Ben Hur, c. 1950.

down there with their towels and they used the river as a bath. There was a boxing booth and they would throw out the gloves to anyone who was prepared to take on the fair men. There was a fat lady, she was huge and we used to pay to go and see her. They had fortune tellers. You could buy sawdust balls on a bit of elastic. In those days the pubs kicked out at ten. They couldn't serve them quick enough so they used to have the beer in big baths, and they'd dip the pint pots in and ladle out the beer. They were three parts to the wind when they came out of the pubs and into the fair, there was always fights. It used to get to midnight and all these coppers used to come round, but the fair people kept playing the music, 'God Bless the Prince of Wales' that always had to be played at the end, but they kept playing it over and over so they could get another ride in. They kept going to past midnight and the music was really loud, each ride had its own organ, and they were all playing different tunes. The music was beautiful. They didn't have electric light in the early days, they had what they called 'goose' flares. *Doug Flitton*

My grandmother lived in Myrtle House along Regent Street. She always wore black, long dresses, everything black, and she loved her pickled onions even though she was getting on for ninety. She'd make jars and jars of pickled onions. Anyway at Stotfold Feast my grandmother used to store cycles in her yard and she would charge about a penny. I've seen up to a hundred bikes in her yard. Grandma would stand there watching everyone pass by.

At the Feast there was a dark man who could do wonderful things with his tough feet, and he used to get a red hot iron and kick it with his bare feet and tread on broken glass, and also he would lick the red hot iron. What he'd got on his tongue I don't know, but us boys were very impressed by that. You could buy a bag of confetti for a ha'penny and also a penny squirt which was kind of a toothpaste thing made of lead and filled with water. The idea was you got this and squirted down the girl's neck and then rammed the confetti down the back of her dress. That was great fun and a good way of meeting girls. *Claude Ingrey*

At the Feast one time these old boys put all this confetti down the front of my dress and it was all wet. *Mill Dear neé Smith*

One year my sister and I had made ourselves new collars for our dresses, especially for the Feast. We'd walked to Baldock market and bought this red material, well honestly and truly it was only 6d a yard. Well, the lads squirted us with water and all the red ran on to the white of our dresses. I think the Cake Walk was everybody's favourite, especially the elderly people. They'd have a few drinks at night and muck about on it. *Florence Phillips neé Gentle*

Lewellyn was the Rock King what used to come in from Peterborough. He was the first and he had a big old sombrero hat and a waxed moustache. He had buckets on the counter for his cash and he'd stir this old cash up and say quarter-pound of this, quarter-pound of that, half-pound of this, so much the lot. And they'd be standing all round the front. After he died Reynolds took over. At the same time that the Rock King used to come in, there used to be Tilley's from Bedford, they were sweet makers. There was also a hot pea stall in there by the name of Frank Holland. Well, he used to stand down that bottom end where my stall was – the Coach end as we called it. He had a big old fire, one of these 40 gallon drums halved and he had a couple of good old pots with these peas in, they'd be boiling away there. He had a little marquee effort and you could sit down and have these peas, 4d I think, a bowl. In the early 30s there used to be two sets of gallopers, then two sets of carousels; one was Harris's, and one was Mannings, and also the Cake Walk that used to stand at the top end. Also there was an old set of gondolas; you can see a set at the museum at Fakenham; that's the only set left in the country. It was big cars that used to go up and down the hills, just like big chariots but they were beautifully decorated and carved. Us old boys used to sit on the steps of the galloping horses as they went round. We'd have a go at the old coconut shy, of course things were a penny then, penny a time which wasn't so bad. A shilling used to go quite a long way. I used to save up for the fair, that was the big event of the year in Stotfold. *Reg Saunders*

Stotfold Feast night there would be somebody come round with a basket of fish and great old lumps of bread. You bought a bit of fish and they slapped it on this lump of bread for you. *Biffy Charles*

When it was just the Mannings and Harris's at the Feast they used to fight and argue, we never had no sleep all the week, they were terrors. Were we pleased when Thurston came and took over! Whenever Mr Thurston came to mark out The Green he would come in here and have a cup of tea with me. He wouldn't mark The Green unless he had his bowler on. He did it so that there were no arguments between the showmen. He always used to smoke a cigar. *Phyllis King née Brown*

In the early 30s, after school on the Monday subsequent to Feast week, many of the older boys would make their way to the deserted, litter-strewn Green recreation ground. They would obtain tin cans about the size of a cocoa tin and make holes in the bottom to allow the passage of air. The cans would be filled and replenished with old pieces of coconut tufts and other combustible material left from the feast. This would be set alight with a match. Lengths of wire would be fixed to the top of either side of the tins making loops about 20 inches long. These wire loops were used not only to carry the hot tins around but also to whirl the cans round and round overarm to get the fire really going. In those days penny squirts, which resembled small plain lead toothpaste tubes and were filled with water, were sold at fairs for people to squirt one another. The used lead squirts were picked up from the ground by the boys and put into small tin cans. These were placed

The Saunders' fish stall at the Feast.

Above right: Liberal Club outing, c. 1921.

Below right: Stotfold Conservatives visit the Houses of Parliament. Mr Alan Lennox-Boyd, MP, in the background.

on top of the tin cans with the fires in them and in this way the squirts were melted down to make lumps of lead. This whole procedure is not something that would be recommended today. *Bert Hyde*

As well as the excitement and enjoyment that the Hospital Demonstration and the Feast brought, the people of Stotfold were also entertained by the yearly visit of the circus, a travelling theatre, and wrestling which all took place in the Pig and Whistle meadow.

Chipperfield Circus used to come into the Mixies field. One day, during a very wet season, the ground was very wet underneath. This particular time, Chipperfield's turned up with a great engine and rode straight onto the ground and it sunk right into the ground. I will never forget it, there must have been hundreds of kids all pulling the rope to help pull the engine out. We got it out eventually, it was great fun for us. That used to be quite a big show. There was a fella' named Scoot and one named Clement, they used to set the stage in front of the show and they had great big electric lights that they generated themselves. I can see them now dancing along that stage to attract the crowd. As far as I can remember, the circus used to come before the Feast. *Bert Jeffs*

Besides the circus there used to be a travelling theatre come into the Pig and Whistle medda'. They erected sort of a portable building just inside the medda' there and they stayed there probably for two or three weeks at a time. *Sam Pooley*

The wrestling booth used to be in the Pig and Whistle medda', that's where Charlie Keeper took on some real class stuff in that tent. People would come for miles to watch this wrestling. *Biffy Charles*

General Elections

The political history of the Mid-Beds Constituency, of which Stotfold is part, is easy to summarise. Up until 1933 it was held by either a Liberal or Conservative; since then it has been held continuously by the Conservatives. Labour has never really challenged, except in 1945 when all three candidates finished close together, with the Conservative winning. Most people, of whatever political persuasion, agree that elections are not now the fun they used to be.

Jim King lived in Tythe Cottage, he had a smallholding opposite the cemetery. He had a two-storey barn there; he used to put his potatoes underneath and his onions up the top. Him and his father, they didn't always get on very well, because Kingy was a very staunch Liberal and the old man was a Tory. It was all Liberals and Tories then. They used to have a lot of political arguments. When

Liberal Club Dinner.

there was a general election, Kingy and the old man were constantly arguing. Kingy went to work one morning to work on his ground and somebody had written on the side of his barn in red paint, 'Vote for Prothero'. Well Prothero was the Tory candidate. Of course, he straight away blamed the old man for it. But he denied having anything to do with it. Some years later I was talking to the old man and I asked him, 'Did you put that slogan on Kingy's shed?' He said, 'No I didn't, but I supplied the paint'. *George Turner*

In the old days Parliamentary election meetings in Stotfold were better attended and more lively than they are today. There was more heckling and witty exchanges. Everybody attended everybody else's meetings and there were many cries of 'rats' and 'rhubarb'. In a crucial General Election in the early 30s the sitting Liberal member, Milner Gray, and his Conservative opponent, the young Alan Lennox-Boyd, later Viscount Boyd, fighting his first election in Mid-Beds, had arranged meetings in Stotfold at the same time – both clubs were in the High Street, and on the night, both halls were crowded. Milner Gray turned up on time and spoke at his meeting, but Lennox-Boyd failed to arrive for his. After a time, many of the crowd from the Conservative Club moved along to the Liberal meeting making it a very large gathering indeed. Milner Gray had finished speaking and just left the hall when who should appear on the scene but Lennox-Boyd, complete with blue rosettes. Jimmy Hallworth, secretary of the Liberal Club and later Stotfold's County Councillor, invited Mr Lennox-Boyd to address the meeting and he did so, standing on the billiard table because of the crush. Mr Lennox-Boyd, who won the election and represented Mid-Beds for many years, never forgot the incident, and every time he came to Stotfold for election meetings for years afterwards would make reference to the time he had spoken in Stotfold Liberal Club standing on the billiard table. To which a voice from the crowd replied, 'Yes, and it has never played true since'. *Bert Hyde*

We used to call ourselves the 'True Blues'. We had a dancing troupe for sketches and things. We went round and entered various competitions, we won lots of cups. Lennox-Boyd was around in those days. We always used to perform in the Conservative Club along the High Street, and in other villages. When there was a political meeting and people were coming to speak, we would keep everyone entertained before the speeches, they were always late arriving. At these meetings there were always crowds of people around the sides, heckling, I used to love it. I did a sketch once called, 'Bill and Harriet at the football match', John Bigg was Bill and I was Harriet. *Dorothy Pond née Nisbet*

Below: The True Blues.

Chapter 11

Stotfold at War

The Boer War 1899–1902

There were few men from Stotfold who volunteered to serve their country in this war, but, by the time those who did arrived in South Africa, the war was already over.

I don't remember the South African war, but I've heard talk about it. When the soldiers used to come home they would arrive at Arlesey Station and more often than not the people knew they was coming. But if they didn't the soldiers would wait in the Fox and Duck and have a couple of pints while the parson organised the band. They used to take the band along there and play them home into the village with, 'Lo, the conquering hero comes'. *George Turner*

The First World War 1914–1918

As the start of the First World War is almost 80 years distant, it is not surprising that few first-hand memories have been recorded. Most families would have been affected in one way or another and, although exact details are not known of numbers serving in the forces, the absentee votes list for 1918 shows that at least 219 Stotfold men were serving away from home.

There was no conscription in 1914, so army officials travelled from village to village encouraging men to enlist. The Biggleswade Chronicle reported one such meeting, held on The Green on 18 September 1914. A crowd had been gathered, pied-piper like, by a small band of bag-pipers playing military airs through the streets leading to the recreation ground. County Councillor J. N. Saunders chaired the meeting saying they had, 'met at a time of great struggle, when none were for party, but all were for state'. Also at the meeting, the Lord Lieutenant commented that 'If he knew anything about Stotfold (people) they valued their freedom and independence.' He then urged the young men to enlist for the new corps of Bedfordshire Territorials that was being formed – and two were so persuaded.

The women of Stotfold also did their bit for the war effort, many travelling to Letchworth to work in the Kryn and Lahy factory making shells.

Bruce Pateman on his horse, wearing the uniform of the Beds. Yeomanry. Horse held by Arthur Castle.

But it was a tragic time for many Stotfold families, some of whom lost more than one relative as the full list of those killed in action shows: Archie Allen, Harold Allen, Edwin Auburn, Alfred Bass, William Bandy, Wilfred Brown, Bert Bygrave, Bernard Bygrave, William Bygrave, Ernest Bygrave, Sidney Bygrave, F Bonfield, John Carter, William Chapman, Cornelius Chapman, Ernest Childs, Robert Clarke, Cecil Cooper, Ernest Cooper, Thomas Cooper, Bernard Cox, Harry Cox, James Cox, R Davies, Ernest Dear, Sidney Dear, William Dear, Daniel Gentle, Ernest Gentle, Sidney Gentle, Bernard Gentle, Frank Gentle, Jack Giddings, A E Godman, Ernest Hancock, Peter Hewitt, Ernest Howard, George Howard, Alfred Huckle, William Huckle, Walter Huffer, Clifford Kitchener, W Langford, Thomas Larkins, Alfred Millard, Harry Nickerson, William J Osborne, E Payne, V Payne, W Payne, E Rollins, F Pidgeon, E Porter, W Reynolds, H Sanderson, H Smith, H Stapleton, Alfred Triplow, Harry Triplow, William Triplow, Wilfred Triplow, Horace Triplow, F Turner.

One day when I was at school, from half past eight till six o'clock at night, troops went right through Stotfold; there must have been 200 bands that day. The first one that came through was a horse regiment, 200, 300 horses and a band in front of that. That would go, then another couple of seconds after coming down Baldock Road would be another lot, same thing again, band in front and soldiers marching; this kept up all day. I've never seen anything like it in all my life. When we finished school, we followed them all the way to Shefford and as we came back they were still marching past.

Sometimes soldiers used to camp overnight in Cook's meadow. One night there would be horse trailers in there, then the next night there would be perhaps a thousand motorbikes come in, they always had little tents. Every night there was something that was interesting to us old boys.

One day all the people of Brook Street went and stood on the allotments near the Stag to watch a Zeppelin go over. It dropped a bomb at Willian, it only had one. Then the Zeppelin come down on a railway line at Cuffley. We saw it flare up, explode and fall down. A piece of shrapnel from the bomb at Willian knocked a window out of a house and made a hole in the wall. They charged sixpence to go and see it. We biked over there to have a look. There were only two Zeppelins that came over Stotfold during the war. *Wally Larkins*

Top: Albert Scott, Royal Navy Air Service. Lost at sea with eight people in an airship disaster, November 26, 1917.

Above: Albert (Paggy) Triplow, Beds. Regiment.

I know it was a long while ago, but what sticks in my mind is hearing my mother say, 'Shut that door, there's a Zeppelin about'.

There was a lot of activity in the village. There was a unit of Canadian signals billeted up the Unionist Club. There used to be a nice oak fence in the front of the club, with double gates in the middle, all their cables and vehicles were parked behind this fence. They used to go laying wires in different parts. One time I went with them to 'inxworth, I weren't very old, cause I was born in 1912. The carriage they had was like the old-fashioned timber carriage with one pole going up the middle connecting the two lots of wheels. They put their rolls of cable on this carriage. They'd string the cable along the telegraph poles, they didn't make nothing tidy. They was laying wires all over the show.

I remember airplanes coming about 'ere. On one occasion a little single seater, one of ours, come down in Norton Road opposite Moses corner. He 'ad to land. *Archie Shepherd*

For a time the rationing in the First World War was worse than the Second. If I remember rightly each person was allowed 8oz of sugar, 6oz of margarine or butter, 2oz of lard, 4oz of jam, 2oz of cheese, 2oz of tea, then there was a shillings-worth of meat, plus bacon and ham in varied amounts. That was your weekly ration. *Olive Chapman née Oliver*

Below left: John Huckle and comrade, Beds. Regiment.

Below right: War wound notification.

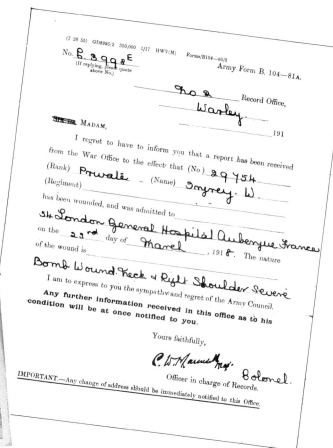

Second World War 1939–1945

During the First World War families had to endure the loss of loved ones and at times cope with severe shortages. Some women were called upon to do war work, but the majority of those left at home were able to carry on their day-to-day living in much the same way as before. The 1939–45 war had a much greater impact on every day life as those who were not called up had to work either on the land or in munition factories unless they were in a reserved occupation. And at the end of a day's work still more was asked of them on the home front in the Home Guard, ARP or auxialliary fire service or as special constables, first aid workers and nurses.

Life was especially hard for women with young families; not only were they now without the help and support of their husbands, but they had to cope with food shortages by concocting nourishing meals from a meagre weekly ration.

Evacuees were an added worry – they were, for the most part, not used to living in a rural community and both sides had to adjust to the new situation.

But those who endured the most were the fighting men and, as in World War I, some never came back – G.T. Cooper, R. Charles, D. Childs, C.J. Carter, A.G. Gyngell, W.T. Howells, W. Robinson, A.J. Smith, B.F. Smith, F.L. Scott, B.I. Thomas, J. Willescroft.

Basil Smith, Royal Airforce, bomber pilot, who received a Distinguished Flying Cross for his brave endeavours in the 1939–45 war.

My father, who served in the army in the First World War, was a special police constable during the Second. His main job was patrolling the streets of the village at night to see that the 'black out' regulations were being complied with. All windows had to be screened to prevent any light showing. Road lamps, including bicycles, had to have a mask consisting of horizontal louvres which ensured that light could not be seen from above. He also patrolled during the day-time if the air-raid siren, which was on the roof of the Regent Cinema, sounded the alert. It gave short blasts for an air-raid warning and a continuous blast for an 'all-clear'. His other duties included helping with traffic control, when convoys of army vehicles passed through the village, and assisting the Red Cross and St John's ambulances in carrying wounded service men to the Three Counties Hospital from Langford siding where the hospital train was put for safety from the main railway lines. *Claude Ingrey*

I went to work up the Three Counties 'ospital in October 1936, still in the building line, like, there weren't much work about then. If you worked in them places at that time you was forced to join their ARP system or fire brigade. The male nurses used to have to do that, and when war broke out they clobbered some of us for it. I had to turn out every time the siren went, and if it went off at night when I was at 'ome, I had to get me bike out and get up there. Eventually they got some beds so that we could sleep there at night.

The military had some tents put up there, big marquees with wooden floors, they put 'undred beds in each one. We had some trains come into Langford siding with a few hundred wounded French soldiers. There was Green Line buses that come there to pick 'em up from the trains, like. There was nine come in each bus. Our job was to get the stretchers and carry 'em in off the buses. There were some poor sorry sights I can tell you. Then I went in the army in 1942. *Archie Shepherd*

During the war I worked at the Royal Free which was transferred from London to the Three Counties Hospital. My job was assisting one of the almoners. I had to handle all the money. There were quite a few almoners up there because it was terribly busy then. In those days people had to pay to come into hospital. They were all assessed by the almoners and I had to go round the wards collecting the money.

We would often bring soldiers in wheelchairs back to our house to tea, just to give them a treat and to get them out. We had very good times up there, we had all sorts of parties and dances. We used to get the soldiers stationed at Radwell to come to our dances. Vera Lynn came to sing at the Three Counties once. Our house was always full, mostly nurses from the Royal Free, who were lodging with us. *Dorothy Pond née Nisbet*

There were a lot of soldiers up at the Three Counties, that's where I met my husband Joe. He come from Dieppe with the wounded up there. When he was first up there he had to wear a red jacket and coat. The wounded came from all over, and when they were better they were sent back to their regiments. The Japanese prisoners of war was all sent up there. *Peg Humphries née Millard*

I served in the Home Guard. We used to turn out on the siren at first and sit on the kerb side in the moonlit nights. When the all clear went we could go home. By the time we got home the siren went again. We used to go to Arlesey station and go along and inspect the bridges through to Langford and then go back to the bridge at the Three Counties. On one occasion Freddy Trussell was with me, and when we got back to the Liberal club I called them together for inspection. Freddy took off his overcoat and threw it down, quite forgetting that he'd got two bombs in his coat pocket!

We used to have to go on top of the church, that was when the real bad raids were going on in London, and you could see the fires. There was Deany, Harold Smith and Frank Kitchener who used to all go on together. We weren't allowed to take a rifle or anything through the church and we weren't supposed to take drink. Well, Lieutenant Busby went round there one night because he'd heard a noise. They were only taking the rifles up the church tower on a rope and their beer up as well. All those boys used to love to drink. Dad's Army all over again! *Jack Brown*

Top: The Home Guard marching along High Street.

Middle: Stotfold Auxiliary Fire Service, 1941. The fire tender was adapted by the men from an old Austin 12 chassis at a total cost of £15.

Below: Special constables in the 1939–45 war.

George Day asked me to join the Home Guard to help him out with the office side. Well, it was Tuesday and Thursday night and Sunday mornings. Evening meetings were 7.30 to 9.30. You bear in mind I was only about 16 and that meant I left work at six o'clock. I had to wait for the bus, I'd get home at seven, my mum used to have the tea on the table to choke myself with, and then Freddy Brown or Gentle, or Alfie Oysten, used to give me a cross-bar up to the Liberal Club.

We used to have map-reading, drilling, all the sort of things you needed to know if it came to a conflict, and knowing how to fire the guns. We did the live firing up near the cemetery.

My dad used to do fire-watching. There were many nights he'd be called out. Up he got, alarm in one hand, shoes in the other, he daren't put the light on, then the clock would fall down the stairs, then they'd be a few sweet nothings. He would sometimes get up as much as three or four times a night. Then he had to do his job on top. There was no days off because you'd been up all night. *Hilary Saunders née Devereux*

My father was absolutely broken-hearted when war broke out again. He actually thought they'd been in one war and it was a war to end all wars, and he quite thought we would be gassed and everything else. He made mother put blankets up at the bottom of the stairs and all the pails ready to damp them. *Florence Phillips née Gentle*

I had to have evacuees in during the war. I had trainees from Ascot Skill Centre, and then when Jack was away I had Land Army girls. Most of the people who stayed were pretty good. My brass bedstead I gave it up to help the war effort, that was quite a sacrifice. They were asking everybody. They took the railings from in front of the cemetery and lots of other places. *Lily Edmonds née Huckle*

During the war there were about 27 people working at the wood-yard. There must have been five German prisoners and Dad used to take them back to the camp that was on Royston Heath, and fetch them every morning. We also had five Italian prisoners, Giovanni, Rapini, Pedro, Celeste and one more whose name I can't remember. Otto was a big German doctor, and every day Dad and Otto used to go down to the old brewery, pick up the old bags of oats after they'd made the beer, and they used to have two pints each. The Italians originally stayed with us and mother used to look after them, but in the end they used to look after themselves. Father used to get spaghetti in one hundredweight sacks, I don't know where they got it from, but because they were prisoners of war they could get it. And they would go up to Floody's because they were allotted ten cigarettes a day. They always said that the prisoners of war lived better than the people in Stotfold. *David Shepherd*

Below: Service of dedication for those who lost their lives in the Second World War. Unveiling of the memorial by Harry Johnson, with the Army Cadet Corp in attendance. The Army Cadets played a very important role during the war, working alongside the Home Guard.

Chapter 12

Reflections of the past

Over twenty years ago Madge Keeper neé Rowley wrote this wonderful description of Stotfold as she remembered it. Her vivid memories are of a picturesque country village, which sadly no longer exists.

I was born in Bedfordshire, in a long straggling village called Langford; this village was also the place where my father was born, but, as we moved to Stotfold when I was only a year old, this being the home of my mother and her people, my roots grew there in very pleasant surroundings.

Like most villages, Stotfold had its 'ends', I lived at the 'top end', where the High Street curved through meadows bordered with great horse-chestnut trees, whose red and white blossoms in the spring rivalled those of any tropical island. Then there were the tall lime trees, dripping their sweet nectar, and filling the air with their heady perfume. A little further along were the walnut trees; these were fair game for all the children of the village, and it was a very irate farmer who would chase us off if we dared to climb through his fence to pick up any nuts that had fallen in his meadow; but as the branches overhung the road, we were usually able to fill our pockets, especially after a strong wind.

Brook Street, where I lived, branched off the High Street and almost the first building was the shoe mender's house. By the side of this was a brick hut where he used to mend his shoes (Dick Strike). In this hut, was a little iron stove which he kept burning day and night. Along the walls were wooden forms, and from the beams in the ceiling hung leather thongs, tools, shoelaces, and all the equipment needed for mending shoes. Last but not least, up one corner was a glass-fronted cupboard. It was the contents of this cupboard that brought children from all ends of the village to sample its contents. For a ha'penny, the old cobbler would fill a half-pint bottle with water, then, after asking which flavour was wanted, would drop a pellet of the required choice in the bottle. This pellet would start to fizz as soon as it touched the water. As it sank to the bottom of the bottle, it left a trail of glowing air bubbles in its wake, fizzing its way down like an astral comet, and turning the water into a sparkling ruby or topaz, according to whichever flavour had been chosen.

High Street, c. 1914, with Stotfold House in the background.

Brook Street.

For a penny, a whole pint bottle could be bought. This needed two of the wonder pellets, so if we were lucky enough to be able to afford one of those, two different flavours would be chosen, which gave a rainbow effect as the bubbles raced upwards. These magic bottles of drink, went under the name of 'monsters', so, having acquired our ha'penny or penny 'monster', we would seat ourselves on the forms ranged round the walls, prepared to stay the evening, especially if it was cold and wet, as there were never less than 10 to 15 of us. I look back and wonder what manner of man the old cobbler really was, he must have loved children, as I never once heard him forbid any of us to enter. There he would sit, a slightly-built little man, his shoulders hunched over the hobbing foot that he held between his knees, deftly driving brads, which he had been holding in his mouth, into the shoes, his silver hair standing out in wisps, and when the little stove was burning well, it would reflect in his steel-rimmed glasses, giving him the appearance of a little gnome.

Opposite the cobbler's house was a cherry orchard, this was entered by a white five-barred gate, flanked by two weeping willow trees. Then came my grandfather's house, this was built of mellow buff bricks, and was unique in that the hall was built in the centre of the house, so, of course, this was windowless. I remember my grandfather once showing me a large map of England, and telling me it was printed long before the railways came, and of how, when he was a boy, there were only houses with thatched roofs in the village.

Grandfather, whose name was Rowley, had eleven children, so I was not without plenty of aunts and uncles. Going down from grandfather's house were other cottages, each nestling in its own little flower garden, then came the Primitive Chapel; this, like most chapels, stood square and ugly, surrounded by high iron railings. Almost next to this was a row of thatched cottages, which would have done justice to any Walt Disney film. They were floored with red quarry tiles, and each one had a huge inglenook fireplace, the little bedroom windows peeped out from under thatched gables, where most of the time peacocks could be seen parading, their beautiful feathers glinting like rainbows in the sunlight. Lilla's bungalow came next, a typical picture-book house, with the heavily thatched roof curving over the door, then rising steeply to form a tall gable. Lilla suffered from a weak heart, so some days she would send me up to the grocers, who also sold wines and spirits, (Westrope's), with a medicine bottle for two shillingsworth of brandy. This, between sips, she would carry in the capacious pocket of her snowy white apron. Then I would help her empty her beetle traps, these were jam jars filled with sweet water, which she placed round the old chimney piece. Apparently the beetles tried to drink this and fell in head first and most days the jars were full up. Sometimes she could be heard singing in a

Mill Lane, leading to Randall's Mill.

Regent Street, c. 1910.

tremulous voice across the garden, 'Hark, Hark my soul', I never heard her sing anything but that, and even today, whenever I hear it sung, I think of dear old Lilla.

Next came our house, a pleasant little red brick cottage, whose four heavily laced windows looked south into the sun, across the field, green in the spring but later to turn to gold as the corn ripened. One of these fields had 'a rare gift for growing rubbish', as the farmer so aptly put it. Consequently, each year there blazed forth several acres of scarlet poppies, with masses of blue scabious jostling for places among the corn, making a picture which no artist could hope to rival.

A few more cottages lay between ours and the old Pig and Whistle, a typical pink-washed country pub, the brook which gave the street its name, lapped round its gardens, while the front faced on to the meadows, known locally as the Mixes. In its great yard strutted dozens of hens, white leghorns, and those hens which had black feathers, speckled with white, and bright red combs on their heads.

On most summer evenings, a metallic ring could be heard as the quoit found its mark in the game being played in the yard, humour flashed like sparks, which had merged into a pleasant drone by the time it reached us in the meadows.

Lazily the village wound its way down to The Green, as it was known, and if you didn't want to go by way of the road, you could take the path which led through the meadows, where in the middle of one was situated the brewery. On the days when they were brewing, a pungent smoke would issue from its tall chimney, and the smell of boiling malt and hops would pervade that part of the village which was to windward of it.

On The Green itself, the annual fair was held, this was known for miles around as 'Stotfold Feast', and was a notable event in that part of the county. Excitement mounted as the great steam engines hissed and puffed their way towards The Green, their huge iron wheels ponderously turning, as if to hide their latent strength, their glinting brasses throwing out swords of light in the sunshine. Majestically they puffed on, pulling in the wake, gondolas, cakewalks, and flying horses, such as never graced any meadow, wonderful was the music, seemingly churned out of the very heart of the roundabouts, and even when the last hard-saved penny had been spent, there was always plenty to watch, such as spit rock being made, and strong men, scantily dressed, flexing their muscles in an attempt to lure people into their tents. When it was all over, how desolate The Green looked for a while, with only the wheel marks to show where the great engines had stood.

Round The Green itself, clustered cottages of various shapes and sizes, some with thatched roofs, others with slates or pantiles, blending gracefully with each other, and making a pleasing picture. It was past this end to the village that the River Rhee flowed leisurely through fields and meadows, from its source three miles away in the watercress beds, its waters were very cold, having sprung so recently from the earth, but had the advantage of being clean, as there were no drains or ditches to empty into it, at least until it had left Stotfold.

This river started work early in its career as, two miles from its source, it set the machinery of Randall's Mill working, how, I don't know, as there was no waterwheel visible. From there it meandered through tree-shaded banks to Blue Corner, here it spread itself out, its waters forming a huge mirror, which on sunny days reflected the blue sky. Golden Corner was its next objective, when tree-shaded banks were left behind as it curved its way through sunny meadows to Bowman's Mill, passing unhindered by Taylor's Mill, this mill having been idle for as long as I could remember.

Bowman's Mill lay in idyllic surroundings, with lush meadows on either side, while tall trees encircled it, as if protecting it with their spreading arms. In the yard was an iron grating, and, by turning the wheel that stood by the side of it, the miller was able to divert the course of the river. When this was done, the river would pour down under the grating in a thunderous waterfall, seemingly into the bowels of the earth, emerging on the other side of the yard to sport with the massive waterwheel that hugged the mill wall.

Reprinted with permission from 'Bedfordshire Magazine', Summer 1971, publisher White Crescent Press Limited, Luton.

*   *   *

Through the pages of this book we have attempted to bring back a few of those happy memories from the days when the sun always shone! In reality, times were often tough and life was harder, yet people appeared to be content with less and faced each day with a resolute, neighbourly spirit.

As we look over our shoulder at these bygone years, it is apparent that we can still learn a lesson or two from our local forefathers. I wonder how our heirs will remember the Stotfold residents of the 1990's?

John Street

The Green.

Allotments

Common Road

B.M 142·6

Fen H

Crown
(P.H.)

Rises

Recreation
Ground

Manor
Lodge

Allotments

B.M

Brewery

F.P.

Rooktree House

DARK LANE

Head
(.)

160

L.B

Reho
Chap

Meth. Chap.
G.P

162·2

Stotfold
House

Shefford 5
Baldock 2¾
M.S

School

THE AVENUE

F.P.

CH

F.P.

CHURCH LANE

F.P.

P.O.

B.M. 148·3

148

Brook End
Recreation
Ground

L.B

Allotments

Black Lio
(P.H.)

F.B.

164